Praise for

FROM HERE TO THE GREAT UNKNOWN

One of the Associated Press's 10 notable books of the year

"[Lisa Marie's and Riley Keough's] perspectives appear in alternating sections—a haunting harmony that builds to a crescendo of heartbreak. . . . The memoir's final 80 pages cover her free fall into addiction. . . . Instead of tap dancing around the hard parts, we're drilling into the bedrock. We hear less from Presley and more from Keough, who comes across as level headed, valiant and kind. . . . Keough approaches the episode with respectful levity, the best tool available to members of a dysfunctional family. . . . Presley still gets a word in here and there, and these passages show how determined she was to stand up to her demons. 'Sometimes I feel like there's nothing left, no purpose,' she writes. But 'I have three remaining children, so I fight it, I fight it, I fight it, I fight it, I fight it.'"

—*The New York Times*

"When her actor daughter, Riley Keough, . . . writes that she wants Lisa Marie to emerge from the pages of the memoir as a 'three-dimensional character,' she's not kidding. . . . It's clear that Presley was nothing if not radically honest. It's also striking how Keough seems to almost plead with the reader to understand and love her mother as much as she does. Ultimately, this is a book built on grief: Lisa Marie Presley's for her father and son, but also a daughter's for her mother."

—*The Guardian*

"The book is of two minds: It's an unadorned, conversational memoir that's more matter of fact than gossipy, little interested in preserving what her father's biographer Peter Guralnick once called 'the dreary bondage of myth.' And it's a frank, almost unbearably heavy meditation on grief. . . . Stunningly candid . . . Both women write gracefully about the unbearable, immovable heaviness of grief. Keough's portrait of her mother in her final months is especially indelible. 'I had mistakenly thought she was so strong-minded that nothing could ever truly hobble her,' she writes. 'But of course it could. Enough pain can hobble anyone.'"

—*The Washington Post*

"Taken from recordings her mother left behind, Keough completed this poignant, moving memoir about Presley's life, which recounts Presley's childhood in Graceland with parents Elvis and Priscilla, the crushing grief that followed after the death of her son Ben and more."

—*People* (The Best Celebrity Memoirs of 2024)

"Having Keough's response contextualizes her mother's pain: Lisa Marie is telling this story to not just *us* but those closest to her. In the abstract, writing a book can feel like shouting into a void, but in the case of *From Here to the Great Unknown,* Keough is always listening on the other side."

—*Vulture*

"Openhearted, unmediated . . . a moving portrait of a life lived on the further reaches of the bizarre planet of American celebrity."

—*Kirkus Reviews* (starred review)

"An intimate glimpse of Presley's experiences growing up in the shadow of her father, Elvis . . . This memoir is a beautiful tribute to the enduring power of love and the complexity of human experience through enduring family bonds."

—*Library Journal*

FROM HERE TO THE GREAT UNKNOWN

FROM HERE TO THE GREAT UNKNOWN

A MEMOIR

LISA MARIE PRESLEY

RILEY KEOUGH

RANDOM HOUSE
NEW YORK

Random House
An imprint and division of Penguin Random House LLC
1745 Broadway, New York, NY 10019
randomhousebooks.com
penguinrandomhouse.com

2025 Random House Trade Paperback Edition

Originally published in hardcover and in slightly different form in the United States by Random House, an imprint and division of Penguin Random House LLC, in 2024.

"the bluebird" by Charles Bukowski published with permission of HarperCollins Publishers, LLC, originally published by Ecco in *The Last Night of Earth Poems* in 1992.

ISBN 9780593733882
Ebook ISBN 9780593733899

Printed in the United States of America on acid-free paper

1st Printing

BOOK TEAM: Production editor: Dennis Ambrose • Managing editor: Leah Sims • Production manager: Katie Zilberman

Book design by Ralph Fowler

The authorized representative in the EU for product safety and compliance is Penguin Random House Ireland, Morrison Chambers, 32 Nassau Street, Dublin D02 YH68, Ireland. https://eu-contact.penguin.ie

KODAK 5052 TMX
12
KODAK 5052 TMX
11
KODAK 5052 TMX
10
KODAK 5052 TMX
36
KODAK 5052 TMX
35
KODAK 5052 TMX
34
KODAK 5052 TMX
33
KODAK 5052 TMX
32
KODAK 5052 TMX
31
KODAK 5052 TMX
30
KODAK 5052 TMX
29
KODAK 5052 TMX
28
KODAK 5052 TMX
27
KODAK 5052 TMX
26
KODAK 5052 TMX

the bluebird

there's a bluebird in my heart that
wants to get out
but I'm too tough for him,
I say, stay in there, I'm not going
to let anybody see
you.
there's a bluebird in my heart that
wants to get out
but I pour whiskey on him and inhale
cigarette smoke
and the whores and the bartenders
and the grocery clerks
never know that
he's
in there.

there's a bluebird in my heart that
wants to get out
but I'm too tough for him,
I say,
stay down, do you want to mess
me up?
you want to screw up the
works?

you want to blow my book sales in
Europe?

there's a bluebird in my heart that
wants to get out
but I'm too clever, I only let him out
at night sometimes
when everybody's asleep.
I say, I know that you're there,
so don't be
sad.
then I put him back,
but he's singing a little
in there, I haven't quite let him
die
and we sleep together like
that
with our
secret pact
and it's nice enough to
make a man
weep, but I don't
weep, do
you?

—Charles Bukowski

Lisa Marie's voice will be in this font.

Riley's voice will be in this font.

PREFACE

In the years before she died, my mother, Lisa Marie Presley, began writing her memoir. Though she tried various approaches, and sat for many book interviews, she couldn't figure out how to write about herself. She didn't find herself interesting, even though, of course, she was. She didn't like talking about herself. She was insecure. She wasn't sure what her value to the public was other than being Elvis's daughter. She was so wracked with self-criticism that working on the book became incredibly difficult for her.

I don't think she fundamentally understood how or why her story should be told.

And yet, she felt a burning desire to tell it.

After she'd grown exceedingly frustrated, she said to me, "Pookie, I don't know how to write my book anymore. Can you write it with me?"

"Of course I can," I said.

The last ten years of her life had been so brutally hard that she was only able to look back on everything through that lens. She felt I could have a more holistic view of her life than she could. So I agreed to help her with it, not thinking much of the commitment, assuming we would write it together over time.

A month later, she died.

Days and weeks and months of grief drifted by. Then I got the tapes of the memoir interviews she'd done.

I was in my house, sitting on the couch. My daughter was sleeping. I was so afraid to hear my mother's voice—the physical connection we have to the voices of our loved ones is profound. I decided to lie in my bed because I know how heavy grief makes my body feel.

I began listening to her speak.

It was incredibly painful but I couldn't stop. It was like she was in the room, talking to me. I instantly felt like a child again and I burst into tears.

My mommy.

The tone of her voice.

I was eight years old again, riding in our car. Van Morrison's "Brown Eyed Girl" came on the radio, and my dad pulled over and made us all get out to dance on the side of the road.

I thought of my mom's beautiful smile.

Her laugh.

I thought of my dad trying to resuscitate her lifeless body when he found her.

Then I was back in my car seat watching my mom's face in the rearview mirror as she sang along to Aretha Franklin, our car barreling down the Pacific Coast Highway with the windows open.

Then I was in the hospital, right after my new baby brother was born.

Bombarded by memories, like a corny flashback montage in a movie. But real.

I wanted her back.

The early parts of the book are mostly her voice—in the tapes she speaks at length about her Graceland childhood, the death of her father, the dreadful aftermath, her relationship with her mother, her difficult teen years. She's frank and funny about my father, Danny Keough. She talks openly about her relationship with Michael Jackson. She's painfully candid about her later drug addiction and about the perils of fame. There are times, too, where it sounds like she wants to burn the world to the ground; other times, she displays compassion and empathy—all facets of the woman who was my mother, each of those strands, beautiful and broken, forged together in early trauma, crashing together at the end of her life.

The tapes are raw, with all the starts and stops that people have when they speak. Wherever possible, I wrote it exactly as she said it. In other cases, I've edited my mother's words for clarity or to get at what I know was the root of what she was trying to convey. What mattered most to me was feeling like the end result sounded like her, that I could instantly recognize her in the pages, and I can.

But there are things she doesn't talk about in the tapes, things she didn't get to, especially in the later part of her life. We saw each other five times a week throughout my life, and we lived together full-time until I was twenty-five. Where there are gaps in her story, I fill them in. The greatest strength for this aspect of the book was also one of my mother's biggest flaws: She was constitutionally incapable of hiding anything from me.

I hope that in telling her story, my mother will resolve into a three-dimensional character, into the woman we knew and loved so dearly. I've come to understand that her burning desire to tell her story was born of a need to both understand herself and be understood by others in full, for the first time in her life. I aim not only to honor my mother, but to tell a human story in what I know is an extraordinary circumstance.

Everyone who ever met her experienced a force—passion, protection, loyalty, love, and a deep engagement with a spirit that was incredibly powerful. Whatever spiritual force my grandfather possessed undoubtedly ran through my mother's veins. When you were with her, you could feel it.

I am aware that the recordings my mother left are a gift. So often, all that's left of a loved one is a saved and re-saved voicemail, a short video on a phone, some favorite photos. I take the privilege of these tapes very seriously. I wanted this book to be as intimate as all those hours I spent listening to her, like the nights she'd spend in bed with us listening to coyotes howl.

In his poem "Binsey Poplars (felled 1879)," Gerard Manley Hopkins writes of that set of chopped-down trees, "After-comers cannot guess the beauty been."

I want this book to make clear the "beauty been" that was my mother.

FROM HERE TO THE GREAT UNKNOWN

ONE

UPSTAIRS AT GRACELAND

I felt my father could change the weather.

He was a god to me. A chosen human being.

He had that thing where you could see his soul. If he was in a shitty mood, it was shitty outside; if it was storming, it was because he was about to go off. I believed back then that he could make it storm.

Make him happy, make him laugh—that was my whole world. If I knew something was funny to him, I would do it as much as I could to get some mileage out of it, to entertain him. When we'd leave Graceland, the fans would always shout, "Alvis! Alvis!" in their Southern accents. I mocked someone doing it once and he fell out laughing, just died. He thought that was the funniest thing he'd ever heard.

Another time I was lying in my hamburger-shaped bed—a huge black-and-white fur bed that had steps leading up to it—and he was sitting next to me in a chair, and I looked at him and said, "How much money do you have?" He fell out of the chair laughing. I couldn't figure out why that was so funny.

I was super connected to him. Our closeness was a lot tighter than I have ever let on to anyone in the past.

He loved me dearly and was totally devoted, one thousand percent there for me as much as he could be, in spite of everyone around him. He gave me as much of himself as he possibly could, more than he could give anybody else.

And yet I feared him, too. He was intense, you didn't want him to get angry with you. If I ever upset him or if he was mad at me at all, it felt like everything was ending. I couldn't deal with that.

When he got upset with me, I took it so personally, I was just shattered. I wanted his approval on everything. There was one time I popped my knee, and he said, "Dammit, why'd you go and hurt yourself?"

It devastated me.

My mom was an air force brat. She met my dad at fourteen and her parents allowed it. It was a different time.

Back then, women were admitted into the hospital while they were in labor. They'd get knocked out and wake up with a baby. She went into the hospital looking glamorous, beautiful, and when she came to, she was just handed a child.

My mother told me that she'd thought about trying to fall off her horse to cause a miscarriage.

She didn't want to gain pregnancy weight. She thought that wouldn't be a good look for her as Elvis's wife. There were so many women after him, all of them beautiful. She wanted his undivided attention. She was so upset that she was pregnant that initially she'd only eat apples and eggs and never gained much weight. I was a pain in her ass immediately and I always felt she didn't want me.

I believe in energy in utero, so maybe I already felt her vibe of trying to get rid of me. Eventually she just kind of decided to keep me, but at the time, she didn't have great maternal instincts.

That might be what's wrong with me.

When I was little, I would often watch my mother do her makeup. There were two sinks in her bathroom, and in between them a huge vanity. My mother had more makeup than any little girl could dream of—MAC and Kevyn Aucoin, drawers and drawers of brushes and lip pencils, eye shadows, and the most famous of MAC lip colors: Spice. She would line her lips—the Cupid's bow she loved and that we all inherited from her father—looking into a small mirror on the vanity, and I thought they were so perfect. To me she was the most beautiful woman in the world.

I looked at her and said, "How old are you?"

It was the first time her age had ever been something I'd considered. She laughed and said, "I'm twenty-eight."

How young that was.

My mom fundamentally felt she was broken, unlovable, not beautiful. There was a profound sense of unworthiness in her, and I could never really figure out why. I've spent my whole life trying to work out the answer. My mother was an incredibly complicated person and deeply misunderstood.

In my family, there's a long history of young girls becoming mothers—my great-grandmother, my grandmother, and my mother all had their first babies young, when they were just babies themselves.

As I got older, I remember wishing that I could have been my mother's mother and my grandmother's mother. I began to recognize what all of the young mothers were missing.

I've been told that mine was a sweet birth story. My dad was very nervous, everyone was. They had lots of dress rehearsals, trying to find the quickest route to the hospital. They had done a few test runs and everything was fine. Then Jerry Schilling, one of my dad's oldest friends, who was driving, almost went to the wrong hospital.

Then I was born.

My mom wanted to look good for my dad, so she decided to put on false eyelashes before he came in to see us. But she was still drugged out and glued them to the mirror instead of to her eyelids.

After that there was a press conference—my mom and my dad walked out of the hospital, did their wave, everyone was taking pictures. So the press was always there, right out of the gate, from the day I was born.

Then they took me home to Graceland.

Graceland was built in 1939 by a doctor and his wife, Tom and Ruth Moore. The land had been gifted to the family by the wife's aunt Grace, so they named it after her. Elvis liked the name so much that he kept it when, in 1957, he paid $102,000 for the then-ten-thousand-square-foot house and its fourteen acres.

Back then, the area was still country—there was nothing out there, five miles south of Memphis. Graceland wasn't even part of the city itself until 1969.

In May 1957, Elvis's mom, Gladys; dad, Vernon; and grandmother, Minnie Mae moved in—Elvis came a little later, on June 26, 1957 (there had been renovations to do and he was off filming *Jailhouse Rock*). After Elvis's return from his stint in the army, others came to live there, including Charlie Hodge and Joe Esposito of the so-called Memphis Mafia, Elvis's entourage who were with him at Graceland from sunrise to sunset.

Elvis's grandmother's room was upstairs, but when his mother died, Minnie Mae moved downstairs. Elvis and Priscilla built a nursery upstairs in 1967 when Priscilla became pregnant; that's where my mom's room was.

Compared to mansions now, Graceland doesn't seem like much of one—visitors are often struck by how small it is. But when Elvis bought it, it was not only a mansion, but represented so much more than mere size and acreage. Until 1953, the Presley family had lived in humble circumstances. Graceland was the physical manifestation of the most incredible American dream come to life. Elvis had been a small-town boy in a small-town family mired in poverty, but he'd made it beyond big, miraculously becoming a godlike figure, the biggest star on the planet. Yet he remained a Southern boy who simply got to buy his beloved Mama a big old house.

He was determined to make his new home an opulent place, and what you do, when you're from the South, is move the entire family in—the aunties, the cousins, everyone. When you come up from poverty, your responsibility is to bring everybody with you, and that's what he did.

The house is surrounded by a big rock wall with the famous music gates in front and a guard gate to the right. As you drive up the winding road, four giant white pillars rise in front of you, guarded by a pair of lion sculptures.

The whole place smells like the South, especially in the summertime. There is soft summer air and fireflies at night. Beautiful trees ring the house: magnolias, elms, willow oaks, red maples, pecans, black cherries.

Once you enter through the front door, immediately to the right is the living room with its iconic stained-glass blue peacocks, single TV, and grand piano. In front of you, stairs lead up to Elvis's and my mom's bedrooms. On the left is the dining room, accented by plush floor-to-ceiling drapes above a black marble floor. The kitchen is also on the first floor as is the famous Jungle Room with its shag carpeting and indoor waterfall. Downstairs you'll find the pool room, with its upholstered walls and ceiling. It's another place, like the Jungle Room, to hide out.

Out back of Graceland are the stables, the racquet-ball court, and next to Vernon's office, a swing set that was my mom's.

My brother, Ben, and I grew up going to Graceland on the holidays. At the end of each day, when the visitor tours were finally over, we'd hang out in the house with our family, eating big dinners and running wild, jumping on the couches, playing pool. Though it was open to the public, when we were there, Graceland was just our home. It's a strange and incredible thing to have your family's history preserved forever in the place where it all happened.

It's as though all the life that was lived in that house—all the laughter, the tears, the music, the heartbreak, the love—is still being lived over and over, down the stair-case, in the walls.

I feel my ancestors there.

There are apparently at least six vortices in the world—like Hawaii and Jerusalem—places with an energy that scientifically acts up.

Graceland was like that.

When you were there, you could feel it. You'd feel good, recharged. My dad went there to recharge.

The top floor of Graceland was just his suite and my room, and that's it. The door to the upstairs would usually be shut, and nobody would ever come up there except the two of us. Even as a child I knew this was super special—nobody, aside from maybe a girlfriend, had one-on-one access like that.

Upstairs at Graceland. Just my room and his room. A sanctuary to be with him.

His bedroom had giant double vinyl black and gold doors which opened out to a small hallway, and then just around the corner was my bedroom. When I came upstairs, I had to walk by his bedroom to get to mine. If the vinyl doors were shut, it meant he was asleep. If they were open and I was up to no good, which I often was, I had to sneak by. But whenever those doors were open, I always made sure to look in to see what he was doing. He'd either be watching TV or talking to people or reading.

There was a house across the pasture that my dad had bought for my grandfather. My dad was nocturnal, and once in a while he would wake me up and put me in a golf cart and take me over there to visit Vernon, who was never ready for it. We'd hang out there for an hour or two and then drive back to the house.

I couldn't get away with much when Vernon was around. He was more of an authoritative figure to me. I wasn't close to him. I would avoid him at all costs. I wish I'd had a different relationship with my grandfather. I just kind of hid from him.

Those night rides to Vernon, though, were really just a moment my dad wanted to spend alone with me.

My dad was very Southern.

No one says "goddamn" like a Southern person, in the right way, with the right soul to it, and the right intonation. When it's done right, it's funny. I heard it all the time. My dad and all of his guys said it the same way.

I wanted to go to the pet store, so one night, my dad shut it down and took me there, along with his entourage. We all got to pick a pet. I picked out a little white foofy dog, and my dad picked a Pomeranian named Edmund. A little while later, I was in my room and they had just brought his breakfast up to his room, which they always did. Then I heard "GODDAMN!" so loud. I ran into his room and he said, "That goddamn dog just stole my bacon!" Edmund had jumped up onto his bed, taken a piece of bacon, and run off with it downstairs. He was so fucking mad at that dog. Edmund became my aunt Delta's dog after that.

Other times I'd be up in my room watching TV and I'd hear "GODDAMN IT!" and I'd go along the hallway to his room to find out what was happening.

"GODDAMN IT I can't sneeze—I need to sneeze, and I can't do it!" I remember him saying once, until he finally got the sneeze out.

I had two cupboards full of stuffed animals in my room, and one day I thought I saw something in there—maybe a mouse or a rat or something—and it freaked me out. So, I ran and got my dad.

"Daddy, something's in my room!"

My dad grabbed his nightstick and a cane, went into my room, and shut the door behind him. Then all I heard was a bunch of banging and thrashing noises, and him yelling, "Goddamn son of a bitch!" He was beating the shit out of the stuffed animals trying to find this thing, whatever the hell it was, but it kept running away from him. In the end he killed it, but no one moved it, and I remember there was a bad smell in there for a month after.

Another time I was in my room, another "Goddamn son of a bitch!" this time coming from the front of the house. Then a loud gunshot.

I went running downstairs and found my dad sitting underneath a tree in a lounge chair. A snake had been coming down the tree and was about to bite his foot, so he shot it.

He scared everybody else. People wouldn't laugh if he seemed upset. But I knew him, so those kinds of things were funny to me. He just had a kind of funny anger about him. It made me love him even more.

I had terrible earaches, and one time my dad rushed me in the wee hours of the morning to Dr. Cantor. I was screaming bloody murder from the pain. Dr. Cantor pulled out some kind of device to get the wax out, or whatever it was, and I was screaming so loudly my dad could not take it and left the room. He didn't want to leave, but he also couldn't bear what was going to happen. He was up against the wall in the hallway, completely white. After Dr. Cantor pulled whatever it was out of my ear, my dad picked me up and carried me out.

Later, I had to have a tonsillectomy. My dad was there in the hospital for that, too. I remember being given ice cream—which obviously no child would be upset about—but it was painful to eat anything, so I made some kind of face every time I had to swallow. My dad was sitting next to my hospital bed, just waiting for me to swallow, and then he would start laughing.

He thought that face was so funny.

Her father called her Yisa. He would replace all the *l*'s with *y*'s when he spoke to my mom.

The other night I was rocking my daughter, Tupelo, to sleep, and I found myself calling her "yitty-bitty" and singing to her, *Momma's little baby loves shortnin', shortnin',* and I stopped and thought, *I literally haven't heard this song since I was a baby.* And I realized in that moment that all of these phrases I use, and the things I say to my daughter, are the ways my mom spoke to me. She had gotten them directly from her dad. From the South. And all of them are alive in me. I can hear her saying, "Get over here, goddamn it, and give me some sugar!" She mothers my daughter through me.

Whenever I go to the South and hear the Memphis accent, I feel a longing, a nostalgia for something I never lived. I've never lived in Memphis. But something inside of me has.

Once the gates closed, Graceland was like its own city, its own jurisdiction. My dad was the chief of police, and everybody was ranked. There were a few laws and rules, but mostly not.

It was freedom.

My dad got me my own golf cart. It was baby blue and had my name on the side—a huge deal for me.

There were a bunch of carts. Me and my friends would tear the lawn up with them, crash into each other in head-on collisions or try to "decapitate" them by running into a tree branch. Full-on demolition derby all day long. I would drive one full speed through a fence, and the next morning it looked like nothing happened—the fence was completely put back together.

There was a shed across the lawn in the backyard. My dad would use it for target practice with his rifles and guns, but at some point, for some reason, it was used to store firecrackers. Dad and his friends would take the firecrackers and shoot them at each other. One day Dad lit one on top of a box of them and they all exploded at the same time. The whole shed went up in flames. Sometimes I can't believe no one was killed up there. I don't know how we came out unscathed, I really don't. Maybe there was some divine entity that was watching over that area, that vortex.

Downstairs, there was a room that had cloth on the walls and a pool table, and a bedroom set aside for any vagrant Memphis Mafia guy who was there that night. Charlie Hodge lived in it. David Stanley lived in it, too. That zone had a vortex of its own. There were never-ending cigarettes, dirty magazines, dirty cards, dirty books. I was all about those dirty magazines.

One time my dad threw a stink bomb down the steps into that room and then locked the doors so no one could get out. I followed right along with whatever he was doing. I would play pool with my friends down there, and then we would turn the lights out and throw pool balls at each other, have pool-stick fights in the pitch-black. Play hide-and-seek. It was open season in that room. The land of shenanigans.

I used to run over people's feet with the golf cart and take off. One day I was tearing up the backyard with the cart and someone told me to stop doing it, and I said, "I'll tell my father on you when he wakes up." Another time somebody told me that I couldn't do something when I was on the golf cart and I said, "I'll tell my father that your wife . . ." I wish I could remember what it was I said that his wife had done.

I was wild.

Joe Esposito was one of the few people at Graceland who was stern with me and wouldn't let me get away with anything. He was never afraid of my dad, and he was never afraid of me. He was just one of those people who would say the truth. He'd say, "The grass is dying," or, "Stop chasing the horses and peacocks with the golf cart!"

There were four female chefs at Graceland—two on in the day and two on at night, ready to make everyone anything, all day long. There were always people to be fed—the house was always jumping and the kitchen was a free-for-all—so there was food being cooked constantly and it always smelled like the Old South. There was fried chicken and French fries and hush puppies and coleslaw and greens.

One day I asked for a chocolate cake, and one of the cooks said, "No, your father's sick, he can't have that," and I said, "I'm telling my daddy you're fired."

I was four.

For many years, Elvis's original chefs would cook for us when we were at Graceland. My mom would have them cook everything she loved, all the things she ate with her dad growing up: fried chicken and catfish, hush puppies and greens, banana pudding. When we'd come to town, the staff would always have our golf carts waiting, and after dinner, we'd go outside and wreak havoc on the lawns—we barely ever drove on the roads.

This was a family tradition.

Billy Idol once came to Graceland and my mom was

ecstatic about it. She was an eighties hair-metal head, so Billy Idol and Guns N' Roses and Pat Benatar had been her teen heroes. She and Billy were off somewhere together on the grounds, but suddenly my mom went running in, breathless.

"I just accidentally flung Billy Idol off the back of my golf cart!" she said, laughing hysterically.

Because my dad slept all day, I was on the run. I had two friends with me—could have been Joe Esposito's daughters, could have been my friend Laura, could have been my cousin Deana. I wish I could remember.

I was in a cute little outfit in my golf cart, sitting against the very edge of the seat so I could reach the pedals. I was out back of Graceland toward the trailers where some of my family lived when somebody flagged me down.

"He's up and he wants to see you."

Damn, it's only two or three in the afternoon, he's not supposed to be up yet. Every possible thing I'd ever done went through my head. *What has he found out? Somebody's told him something. I'm gonna kill whoever told on me.*

"We're in deep trouble," I said to my friends. "I don't know what it's about yet, but he wants me right now, which is a problem."

I started crying walking toward the house and my friends started crying, too.

We made our way upstairs. My dad was sitting on his bed in his usual spot. He would always sit in the same place, leaning back on one of those pillows that has arms and moving his leg or shaking his head. He was always rocking.

He told us to sit down, then he pulled out three little boxes. He gave one to me, one to my friend, and one to my other friend.

I opened mine. It was a beautiful ring set with a flower of diamonds. We all got a ring—my one friend got emeralds and my other friend rubies.

It was so beautiful, but I felt so guilty. My conscience was eating me alive. He had just wanted us to hang out with him and talk.

Twenty minutes before my dad was due to walk onstage in Las Vegas my mom told him, "I'm leaving," and he still had to go out and perform.

I was four when they split up. But I remained so close with my dad. I knew how much I was adored, how much he loved me. I knew that he knew that I hated, hated, hated leaving him. Hated, hated, hated going to my mother's new home in Los Angeles. Loathed it. He got a house there to be closer to me.

When I was in L.A., he'd call all hours of the night to talk to me, or just to leave a message on my phone. I was taking piano lessons there at one point, and he would want to hear them, so my mother would put the phone on the piano so he could hear me playing.

I would do anything he wanted. I would sing, I would dance. He always wanted me to sing. I didn't love it, but I knew it made him happy, so I did it. He wanted me to learn "Greensleeves" on the piano, so I did. He could have said, "Chop both of your feet off," and I would have done it.

Just to make him happy.

Dad and his mother, Gladys, had been so close. But she loved him so much that she drank herself to death worrying about him. She just couldn't bear him being away in the army—he went to Germany—and she died because of it. And that left my dad with his demons, self-destructive demons, and he acted out on them.

I have everything in me that wants to numb out, too, and do the same fucking thing.

My great-grandmother Minnie Mae was known as Dodger because if you threw a football or something to her, she'd always dodge it. Dodger was old and always in a rocking chair watching TV with her snuff pipe in her hand. She came out of her downstairs room maybe once or twice a day.

My dad got me a horse. I don't think it was for any kind of special occasion. He was leading me through Graceland on that pony, right through the house. Everyone was excited, making a commotion, and Dodger was shouting, "What the hell's going on out there?" and right at that moment, the horse stopped and decided to relieve himself right outside Dodger's room. It was pretty rare that she would get out of her chair, but she could do it, and she started to get up to find out what was happening in the hallway. My dad panicked.

"We gotta get outta here, oh my God!" he said. "Clean it up quick before she comes out!"

Then it was a mad rush to get the poop off the floor and the horse out of the house. As fast as he could, he guided me around to the front, made a circle, and we snuck out the back door before Dodger could find us.

Dodger had a daughter, Delta Mae Biggs, my aunt Delta. She took care of Dodger, but Delta was also a diabetic alcoholic, so she was a wild card. She had a horrible mouth and was very vocal about everything. She didn't have a lot of good things to say, but she was very, very funny.

Aunt Delta was sort of put in charge of me for a little while, but she couldn't control me. As much as she could tell me what to do, I wouldn't listen. She'd just say, "Yeah, you little son of a bitch," and give up on me.

Aunt Delta always said my cousin Patsy—she was really a double first cousin—was my actual surrogate mom.

One day my aunt Delta and Patsy were having an altercation in the kitchen and Delta pulled out a knife.

"I'll cut your guts out," Delta said.

Patsy said, "Well goddamn get over here and do it," but Delta wasn't really going to do it. That's just how they talked to each other.

My dad had given Delta his Pomeranian, Edmund. He was like her watchdog, became her protector. If you came anywhere near her room, that dog would start barking, growling, going crazy. You could hear her cursing at him to shut up from behind the door. She'd get in her bathrobe and take him out several times a day, clutched in her right arm. Later, once the tours started coming through, she would still walk through the house in her bathrobe carrying Edmund, run into the visitors, and say, "What the hell are you looking at, you sons o' bitches," throw up her middle finger at them, and keep cursing under her breath as she got the dog outside. One time a tourist said, "Aren't you Aunt Delta?" and Delta said, "Oh hell no, she died."

Delta knew how much I loved Elton John. One Christmas she got me some of his records. My dad watched me open the gift, said, "That's nice," and went off through the swinging doors that led from the dining room into the kitchen. I found out later that in the kitchen he said to Aunt Delta, "Why did you get her those records? Who the hell is this son of a bitch that she's wanting to hear?"

"She likes him," said Delta.

Soon after, before one of his shows, my dad met Elton backstage. He needed to meet this person whose records I was listening to. Elton and I have giggled about it ever since.

I finally met Elton a year later, for my ninth birthday. My mother arranged for me to go to his house. He showed me his clothes, his closet, his boots. He was very sweet.

We had tea.

If there was an authority figure around, I tended to instinctively fight it and not want to be around that person. My grandfather Vernon was one of those. He would tell me I shouldn't stay up late, that I shouldn't eat cookies all day and night. I mean he was right, but I didn't care. I didn't like anybody telling me what to do.

When I was in Memphis, I would wake up at Graceland around two in the afternoon and get everybody riled up, ready to go play. I had friends up there, living with my grandparents, or cousins who lived in trailers in the back. I would ask for French fries or grits for breakfast, go get my golf cart, and off we went for the day.

There were times where I would eat French fries for three days straight, or I wouldn't take a bath for ten days.

Eventually my dad would wake up, and I'd get the call that I was to go upstairs because he wanted to see me. I always loved that call. I'd go and hang out with him in his room. He didn't really leave very often. There were enough people up there and enough going on that there was never a moment of boredom. I would just sit up there, and he'd talk to me and ask what I was doing while he watched one of his seventeen televisions or listened to records. Sometimes he'd come down and take us out—he'd shut the theater down in town and take everybody to see a James Bond movie or *The Pink Panther*.

My dad loved to have fun and he loved everybody else

to have fun with him, and he loved to laugh. He was very gregarious in that way: He didn't do it to have an entourage follow him. He was generous because he wanted everyone else to enjoy everything.

He always had my back. I was friends with one of the neighborhood girls, and I spent the night at her house. As I was leaving the next morning, her next-door neighbor, an older woman who was watering her lawn in her bathrobe, knew who I was and started calling me names and bad-mouthing my dad to me, saying, "He thinks he's the king of everything!" I had never heard someone talk badly about him like that, and it affected me. When I got home, I told my dad what had happened, and he said, "Where does she live?" I told him, and he said, "Let's go." We drove up to her house and he got out, walked up to her, fully decked out in one of his outfits. I saw them talk for a few minutes, and by the end, she had asked him to sign a record for her and they took a smiling picture together.

That's the kind of daddy he was.

Graceland was really busy during the day, so that's when my dad would sleep. But at night it was peaceful for him—people would leave him alone. In the evening, if the vinyl doors were open, I would hang out with him but end up getting tired and putting myself to bed. Nobody had to tell me. He wanted to hang out with me and have me around, so he wouldn't tell me to go to bed very often.

But hanging out with him could be a double-edged sword because I also didn't want to stop whatever devious act I was committing.

I had a friend—his girlfriend Ginger Alden's niece—who was a bit of a troublemaker. She was older than me, maybe eleven, and she had a motorbike. *That's freedom*, I thought, *I want one*.

But I got the idea that my dad didn't want me on it. One day, when he was sleeping, Ginger's niece put me on the back of the bike. As we sped through a grassy area at Graceland, there was a laundry line across the lawn. Ginger's niece didn't see it, drove right through it—it got her around the neck and threw us both backward. The bike fell on my calf and the muffler burned my leg really badly.

That night, I was trying to sneak by his room so I could put on long pants instead of shorts to hide the burn. I had almost made it by, I was one leg away from being in the clear, but he caught me. He called me in.

"What's that?" he said.

I couldn't lie to him.

"It's a burn. The bike fell on my leg. . . ."

My dad was quiet and calm, but I could tell that he was so upset with me.

"Let me have your hand," he said, and he smacked it.

I felt like my life was over. I had upset him because I had hurt myself. That's the last thing he ever wanted for me. It wasn't a control thing—he just didn't want me getting hurt doing stupid stuff.

I went to bed shortly thereafter. In the middle of the night, I woke up to find him standing next to my bed. He was holding a puppet, a basset hound, making it mouth the words while he sang "Can't Help Falling in Love" to me.

> Take my hand, take my whole life, too,
> For I can't help, falling in love with you.

When he was done singing, my dad hugged me and said he was sorry.

Upstairs at Graceland is just as Elvis left it—so you can really feel his presence.

Sometimes we would all sleep in his bed. My mom loved being in her dad's bed—it made her feel close to him, and we felt it, too, that closeness. But because

Elvis's bedroom isn't a part of the tour and no visitors are allowed up there, if we woke up late and the tours had already started, we'd be stuck in his room until late afternoon when the tours stopped. We'd have staff members bring food up—usually McDonald's—and just hang out all day.

Trapped in Elvis's bedroom.

My grandmother's hairdryer was still up there so we'd sit under it and pretend we were in a salon.

He had a little plaque on the wall up there with a poem that always broke my heart. It's titled "Why God Made Little Girls":

God made the world with its towering trees
Majestic mountains and restless seas
Then paused, and said, "It needs one more thing,
Someone to laugh and dance and sing
To walk in the woods and gather flowers,
To commune with nature in the quiet hours."
So God made little girls,
With laughing eyes and bouncing curls,
With joyful hearts and infectious smiles
Enchanting ways and feminine wiles
And when He'd completed the task He'd begun,
He was pleased and proud of the job He'd done

For the world when seen through a little girl's
eyes
Greatly resembles Paradise.

While we waited for the tours to finish, my mom loved to go through her dad's books to understand him better. He was clearly searching for a deeper comprehension of the world—most of the books were spiritual or self-help titles, things like *Understanding Who You Are,* and *Sacred Science of Numbers,* and *How to Be Happy,* Kahlil Gibran's *The Prophet,* even Ram Dass's *Be Here Now*—really human things. There were also lots of Bibles. Elvis would underline phrases and write things like "AMEN!" next to them.

When you saw the underlines and the spiritual searching, you got a sense of the fundamentally broken feeling he shared with my mom. He was searching to fix himself, searching for a deeper meaning, something she would then search for in her own life, too.

So often we'd sit up there, and my mom would go line by line, really reading into everything he had underlined, showing us, grasping at straws.

Then security would knock on the door and bring us sausage and biscuits and we'd eat them.

You can still feel him in that room. His spirit is imprinted there.

I have a vague memory of this one conversation we had in that room about a passage that Elvis had underlined. I started to call someone to help me remember it, but realized that there's no one left to call.

They were always out there, the fans, sitting on the fence or in the trees right by the carport. Next door was woods and a church. Creepers could just come in and sit on the side of the fence or sit in a tree outside the fence, and they would, all day and all night, literally just sit there and watch. There were certain watchers who had a monopoly on a certain tree—they'd be there just to watch my dad walk out of the house and into the car. There was nothing we could really do because it was church property. It was forbidden to go into the woods. My dad would not allow it. It was absolutely out of the question.

I wasn't supposed to, but I would drive in my golf cart real fast and close by the fans and yell obscenities at them. "Fuck you! Fucker!" They'd just sit there and smile and wave.

Sometimes a fan would jump the fence, and there would be an all-points bulletin. Security would come find me: "Get in the house, somebody's gonna kill you!"

Once they had the person arrested, I could come back out. There were always so many people at the front gate, at any given time of day, even in the middle of night. Still are, by the way.

I have never seen nobody at the front gates of Graceland, not ever.

Back then they were waiting to get a glimpse of Dad coming in or out, or me, or someone—whoever was in the house.

At some point I had a bright idea. The fans outside always wanted me to take their camera and take a picture of my dad.

"Give me twenty bucks, and I'll take a picture of him," I'd say to the uber fans by the fence. Sure enough, they would give me twenty dollars, then I would go into the house and take a picture of the floor. I'd give the camera back and say, "Here's a picture of the door and the floor." I started doing that regularly.

I took a fan's camera at one point, but I got bored and didn't feel like taking pictures, so I just threw it in the bushes. I felt horrible about it, though I did it more than once. My uncle Vester, who worked the front gate security, would walk up to the office and say, "Lisa's taken someone's camera again, should we try to find it?"

Years later, someone came up to me and said, "You

took my camera when I was at the front gate and you never came back!" I said, "Oh God, I'm so sorry."

I was Eloise at the Plaza.

I'm not proud of it.

Every year we went to Graceland for the annual Candlelight Vigil, which commemorates Elvis's death, a time when thousands of people attend from all over the world.

I must have been around twenty years old this particular year, and I watched as an older fan, one clearly from Elvis's generation, hugged my mom. That fan was there every year, so I recognized her, but this time I was really watching their interaction; I became keenly aware of my mom's body language in a different way, I guess because I was older. And the way that my mom surrendered to this woman's arms broke my heart. In that moment I saw so clearly that she was searching for a parent.

Graceland just brought mayhem. My dad would get bored riding around the place, so sometimes he would say to me, "Get in the golf cart," and with eight, nine, ten carts behind us, he would lead the convoy right out the front gate onto Elvis Presley Boulevard and down the street. People would be screaming and yelling out of their cars.

He got a new motorcycle with a little sidecar on the right side of it, and he was excited about it. He pointed to the sidecar, looked at me, and said, "Get in." We flew out the front gates, around the residential neighborhoods behind Graceland, and then back into the house. He was riding safely, but I was terrified.

Going to his shows was my favorite thing in the world.

I was so proud of him. He would take me by the hand and bring me out onstage, then get walked to wherever his place was on the stage, and I would be taken from him and brought to wherever I was going to be sitting in the audience. Usually with Vernon.

The electricity of those shows. There's nothing I've felt that's been even close to that feeling, ever. *Electrifying* is such a generic word, but it really is what it felt like. I loved watching him perform. I had certain songs that I liked—"Hurt," and "How Great Thou Art." I would ask him to sing those songs for me and he would always say yes.

I did not, however, like having the limelight shone on me or being asked to stand up in front of everybody. In Vegas, during his residency, he introduced Vernon, then looked toward me and I remember thinking, *Oh God oh God please don't.* "Lisa, stand up!" It's not that I wasn't proud or that I didn't love him. I just liked the limelight on him, loved it on him. It was not something that came to me inherently. I absolutely abhorred it.

But in other less public ways, I loved basking in his fame with him.

In Los Angeles I went to school at John Thomas Dye, up in the hills of Bel Air. I still sometimes drive by it just to remember the day my dad came to a parent-teacher conference. I knew he was coming, and I couldn't wait. I could feel the teachers' nervousness and excitement, too. My little student friends were so excited that I got even more excited—everybody was just running around crazy.

Then my dad showed up. He got out of the car and he had on a respectable outfit—black pants and some kind of blouse—but he was also wearing a big, majestic belt with buckles and jewels and chains, as well as sunglasses. He was smoking a cigar. I met him at the car, and I walked up the walkway with him, and I just remember that feeling of walking next to him, holding his hand.

Sometimes when I watch videos of Elvis performing, I think about the fact that if he hadn't done exactly what he did in exactly that moment in time—if he hadn't walked into the right building, recorded the right song, danced the way he did in front of the right person—there would be no Elvis Presley. We probably would have lived somewhere in Mississippi.

I didn't even finish high school in *this* version of my life, so I can't imagine where I'd be in that one. My great-grandfather drove trucks, maybe we would have carried on that tradition. Maybe we would have made furniture in Tupelo.

My mom would have ended up in jail for sure.

In California, when I was with my mother, I had a nanny named Yuki Koshimata. Yuki was a short Japanese woman, and she took really good care of me. She was always there—she wrote to me until the day she died. I would get cards every Christmas, every birthday, even after I got married and had children.

Whenever we dropped Yuki off at her house for her weekend, or her time off, I would scream. I remember being in the car with my mom driving away and I would be screaming at the top of my lungs, watching us drive out of view of her.

I was so attached to her.

Leaving Graceland and flying out of Memphis International Airport to go back to L.A. was a true emotional trauma for me. As soon as I got out of the car in Memphis, though, I would completely transform. I never wanted to leave. I loved everything about it. I loved the weather, I loved the storms, I loved the cold, the sounds of the birds, the fireflies. I loved the people, I loved the smells. One of my favorite snapshot memories—I was around seven or eight—was of getting off the plane in Memphis, looking down, and seeing snow.

There were the times I would be in school in L.A., and I would see a black car pull up, then someone would come to the classroom to get me, and it was to go to see him. They'd put me on a plane and fly to wherever he was. It was usually on a whim—he would tell someone, "Go get her," and then I would get brought to wherever he was.

I waited for that car to show up—it was always a black one, usually a Mercedes or a limousine. I felt like my life was the best life ever whenever that car came around.

Sometimes he would fly back with me. And he would land the fucking plane, too. At the end of the trip he would get in the copilot seat, which made everybody nervous, and announce, "Ladies and gentlemen, please fasten your seatbelts, Elvis is going to land the plane."

I'd think, *Um, can I get off?* and I would tighten my seatbelt as tight as it could go and then I just remember everyone applauding as we landed, because we were alive.

We were alive.

I was supposed to go back to L.A. because I was about to start school.

"Please, ask Mommy if she'll let me stay," I begged my dad.

"I'll call her and ask her," he said, and told me to go wait in my room. I remember pacing outside his doors, in that hallway with the foot-long shag rug. Eventually he came out and hugged me. I heard this kind of wheezing sound. He was crying.

"You can't stay," he said, "she wants you to come home."

My dad didn't talk about my mom in a bad way at all. He did not want me to think negatively of her. In retrospect, they did a fantastic job maintaining a united front and a real friendship bond. There was still a lot of love between them, and they really put on a good front for me. I was very lucky.

So, he didn't want her to look bad, but he was very, very sad. He pulled himself together and said, "You know, your momma's right. You have to go back because you need to start school and she needs to get you ready. I don't want you to go, you know that, but your momma's right, it's the right thing to do."

That wheezing sound never left me, him crying and trying not to let me know it. It showed how much he loved me.

But I wasn't crazy about my scenario. In school once, I picked up a book about Japan—everything was so beautiful there, the architecture, the ponds, and I remember wishing that I could live there. Not that I was ungrateful, but I was lonely in L.A. I wasn't alone, but I was very lonely. I didn't have a lot of friends. So I'd just stare at that book, wanting to live in the pictures somehow. So far away. Another world, another place, another time.

The only thing that saved me was music. I had a little 45 record player and music was the only thing that would take me away. I'd play Neil Diamond, Linda Ronstadt later, and my dad. I remember being in the middle of my floor with the record player in front of me.

That machine and my Snoopy doll were my imaginary friends. Snoopy was everything to me. I loved him so much that his nose broke off and I sewed it back on. I had outfits for him, clothes for each day. He came with me everywhere. He was my best friend. I took him to school because I was scared to be there, and they made me keep him in my locker, which I hated.

But it made it easier for me to be there, knowing he was there, too.

You could always sense my dad's intensity.

If it was a good intensity, it was incredible; if it was bad, watch the fuck out. Step back. He had this magnetism about him. Whatever it was going to be, it was going to be a thousand percent. And when he got angry, everybody would run, duck, and take cover.

There was this one time—I want to say it was during one of his tours, in Tahoe. He would always take the whole top floor of whatever hotel he was in, for him and the entourage. That night he was back in his bedroom, really, really angry, cursing and screaming. Somebody told me to get behind a chair in the main suite and not move. Everyone was trying to hide behind something, to stay out of the fucking way. So I hid and watched as he took things by the handful, by the armful, and threw them off the balcony. He had found his flight path and he was going to fly it until he was done throwing stuff off that balcony.

Eventually, he calmed down, and someone said to me, "It's okay, you can come out now, he wants to see you."

I thought, *He wants to see me?*

I said, "Why was he so mad?"

"Well," someone said, "he ran out of water."

So, I grabbed four bottles of water and I walked into his room.

"Somebody told me you didn't have any water," I said, and he just motioned for me to come give him a hug.

He was respectful, though—he wasn't rude to people, he wasn't an angry person, he didn't live there. Some people full-on live in destruction, others buy some real estate and walk around in anger for a little while. My dad would just visit.

Sometimes my dad would take me to an amusement park in Memphis called Libertyland, and he would close it down for me and all the entourage and their families and friends. He and I would ride on the roller coasters. I loved it.

One of my dad's visits to anger came one time when we were supposed to go to Libertyland. I had invited all my friends, but when I went upstairs the night before, I could hear the wrong kind of tone—this baritone sound, the wrong kind of intensity. I went to my room and could hear loud crashing sounds. He was yelling his fucking head off at somebody. I could hear him saying that we weren't going to Libertyland the next day. I was devastated.

I found out later that he had run out of something again, and he needed to get it before we went—either that or they wouldn't give it to him. So, he hit the roof and called about ten different doctors and nurses until he found someone who would give him a fix. Once the nurse or doctor had administered whatever it was he needed, he was fine. And we went to Libertyland.

I remember sitting next to him on the roller coaster that day—the Zippin Pippin—keeping one eye ahead on the ride, and the other on his gun in his holster, which was on my side. Unless you knew or understood him, that sounds terrible, I know. You might think he was crazy, carrying a piece with his daughter sitting next to him, but he was just from the South. It was just really funny.

So we rode and rode.

That was about a week before he died.

TWO

HE'S GONE

I was always worried about my dad dying.

Sometimes I'd see him and he was out of it. Sometimes I would find him passed out.

I wrote a poem with the line, "I hope my daddy doesn't die."

He had a TV and a chair set up in my room, so he would often come by and lounge in the chair and smoke his cigars. I could wake up at any time and he'd be sitting there. Once, I was with a friend in my room and when he came to my bedroom door, he started to fall. I could tell that he was moving too far to the right, starting to lean, and I yelled, "Go get him!" Me and my friend managed to get underneath him and hold him up until he grabbed hold of something and regained his composure, and then he just went back to his room.

That happened a few times—happy to see me, then the swaying.

And it happened a lot toward the end.

I was sitting next to him in my room watching TV

and I said, “Daddy, please don’t go anywhere. Please don’t die.”

He said, “I’m not going anywhere.”

Then he smiled at me.

I knew that something tragic was coming, which made me feel protective, that I had to watch out for him.

One time I was walking by his bedroom, and he was lying flat on his back. I saw how bloated his stomach was and it terrified me.

A few days later I was in my room with my friends. We were in the hamburger bed, all watching that sad movie *Brian’s Song.* About halfway through the film, I suddenly got really worried about my dad and went into his bathroom, where I found him facedown. He had used the towel rack to hold on to, but it had broken and he’d fallen. I ran downstairs and got Delta; she called for help, and they got him up, gave him coffee, and got him walking. I watched them walk him around the room. He was clinging on to them. At one point his head was hanging down, but once he saw me in the chair, we locked eyes and his whole face lit up. He tried to get away from them to come over to where I was, but I could tell he was going to be sick.

I said, “No, he’s going to throw up.”

So they took him to the bathroom, and sure enough, he got sick.

I didn't say anything. I didn't talk to anyone about anything. I just internalized it all.

One winter at Graceland my dad wanted me to get on a snowmobile with him, but I was scared. He was wild—a wild card, a wild man. But I got on the snowmobile anyway, because he was my dad. He started going down the steepest part of the driveway. He lost control and we started sliding and jumped the curb. We both stayed on somehow and landed on the grass, laughing.

But there was another time that he and some of his other guys went down on sleds, on their bellies, while the wives and kids were standing around watching them. I was at the top of the hill, and I was worried to death because there was no way to stop those sleds, no brakes, no ropes to pull on. I just remember thinking, *What are you doing, Daddy?*

I watched my dad go down on his stomach, and once again, like with the snowmobile, he jumped the curb at the bottom and rolled three times, and then he lay there, completely still. Everyone got worked up, started running toward him, scared that he was dead. As they approached, all freaking out, he flipped over on his back and let out a huge, guttural belly laugh like you wouldn't believe. He thought it was just the funniest thing.

During the days I ran around with a crowd that consisted of my cousins and friends. My grandfather had a girlfriend, Sandy Miller—she lived across the pasture in the house with him. She had three kids, two boys and one girl. The girl, Laura, was my age. She was one of my best friends. My cousin Patsy's daughter, Deana Gambill, was also my best buddy. I was very protective of her, loved her a lot. But Laura and I would viciously fight each other. I would terrorize her, try to get her to eat my makeup. She and I were fighting in my room because I wanted her Barbie case and she wouldn't give it to me.

"Give me that goddamn Barbie case," I said.

"No!"

"But I can't get it, nowhere has it, you better give it to me," I said. There was a statue in my room and I picked it up over my head and Laura started screaming, "Nooooo!" Then her eyes darted to my right and I looked over to see my dad standing there. I quickly put the statue down and tried to act like we were just playing.

"What are you doing?" he said.

"Nothing, just playing," I said.

"Don't kill your best friend," he said. Words of wisdom.

When I was eight or nine, I had a huge crush on one of Laura's brothers, Rory. I was head over heels, painfully in love with this boy for years. Rory was five feet eleven, dark hair, really cute. He had a great personality, and these green eyes, amazing smile. I couldn't even move when he walked in the room. He would tell me he was going to write me letters, and I'd wait and wait. I'd ask Laura to ask Rory if he liked me. I would hang on to anything that he said or did. I thought it was mutual because Rory kissed me maybe once, maybe twice, when we were playing hide-and-seek in the dark, in the pool room downstairs. I kept wanting to play hide-and-seek to see if he would do it again.

He ended up having all these really beautiful girlfriends and I was always so jealous—my God, I couldn't take it. It would break my heart.

When I was around six or seven, I had been at Graceland for the summer and my dad left on tour, so my mom's mom came and picked me up. We flew to New Jersey together to visit with her and my grandfather and my mom's five other siblings in Mount Holly.

I never had a connection to my grandmother. One time I was in the bathtub, and she knelt over to rinse me and her cleavage was showing and there was this giant dark mole on her chest. I looked at it and screamed bloody murder. "Don't you pick me up with that thing you've got right there!"

I had spent the summer with my father where there had been no rules, so I needed to be de-brat-icized, but I wasn't having it. My mom's parents were very much of the mindset that I was nothing special, that I wouldn't be treated as anything special, that I was just like the rest of their family. The change was so confusing that I would often scream my head off. I remember screaming so loud for a good hour that my mom's younger brothers were all laughing at me.

My mom had my grandmother's chilly disposition, which she got from her mother, my great-grandmother.

At some point I had a little cameo, a compact, a perfume thing that I loved. One day I couldn't find it and I was so upset, crying, and everyone was trying to help me find it. Then I remember being in the car and looking down in my grandmother's purse. There it was. I said, "What's that?" She said, "You didn't see anything, it's nothing," and moved her purse away.

I thought, *Oh my God, the bitch stole it from me!*

I know that I acted like a princess sometimes. But it's

strange, because I was—am—filled with self-doubt. It was all very confusing.

Looking back, there was really only one thing I was sure of: that I was loved by my dad.

We had my ninth birthday party in the *Lisa Marie*, my dad's plane. My dad was in the back in his bedroom, and he came out to join everybody standing around singing "Happy Birthday." Charlie Hodge, his sort of sidekick onstage, came over to me, emptied his pockets out on the table, and said, "Take whatever you want." He didn't have a present, so I was just grabbing the money.

At that point, my dad was dating Ginger Alden. He'd had a bunch of different girlfriends and I liked most of them. There was Sheila Caan and Linda Thompson, who I loved. I could tell Linda really cared about me and my dad. When they broke up, he didn't tell me, and I ran up to give his girlfriend a hug, thinking it was Linda, but it turned out to be Ginger. I didn't mind Ginger, but I didn't like her. Nobody did.

She was always very sweet to me—which was an obvious move unless you were an idiot—but I didn't like that she would upset him. I used to eavesdrop on their phone calls. He had one of those old-school phones where the line would light up and you could pick up another receiver. Those conversations would make me absolutely nuts. She wasn't there for him. I could tell that she didn't love him at all. One time he got in a fight with her, and I remember the sound of his Stutz, his favorite car, as it screeched away. Because I knew they had been fighting, when I heard him take off at high speed out of the gate, I was worried.

I remember him asking me, "Have you seen Ginger? Is she around? Where is she?"

"I don't know where she is," I said.

She was driving him crazy, playing him hard. She would be there for him one minute, and then gone. One day I went with her to go visit her family. I didn't tell him I was going, but I told other people, and she wanted to take me so I thought it was okay. When I got back, he was mad, and that wrecked me.

That whole relationship was so tumultuous.

My mom learned from these experiences to put her children before her partners.

Anytime she got a new partner, she'd bring us into the kitchen and say, "Guys, this is [insert name]," and she'd smile and watch as an uncomfortable exchange happened. But she always wanted to see our read on the new boyfriend—she trusted our instincts.

Later she'd say, "What did you think, did you like him?" If we said no, he'd be gone. If he said one wrong thing to us, she would put him in his place.

Later that year, at the end of another amazing summer at Graceland, my dad was once again getting ready to go on tour. There were all those big tour cases lined up by the front door for loading. He was leaving the next day, and I was going back to California to start school.

I was really depressed about leaving, I didn't want to go.

My dad had built a giant racquetball center and my friends and I had been hanging out there, playing around late at night. Really late, well after midnight. I was coming in through the back door just as my dad was coming out and I ran into him.

He said, "Go to bed," and I said okay. I gave him a hug and a kiss, and we both said I love you. Then I headed upstairs and went to sleep.

I woke up in a jolt in the early afternoon and I sensed

panic. I thought, *Something's not right*. It felt like a different type of energy.

It wasn't unusual for me to be woken up by a commotion. One night I had been woken by drilling and pounding and singing and all kinds of stuff going on. My dad had wanted his organ to be brought upstairs so he could play and sing gospel in his room, but it wouldn't fit through his doors, so they had to do all this construction to get it in.

I found Joe Esposito and said, "What's happening with my dad, where is he?"

"Your daddy's sick," Joe said.

"What does that mean?" I said, and started running into his bathroom, which was absolutely enormous, so big it had a wash bin just for his hair. The shower was gigantic, too, a walk-in, and it kind of wrapped around. There was also a huge closet with a bed in it, for somebody who wanted to take a nap, I guess. It had two entrances, one connected to my room.

I ran across the bathroom and there he was. Just as I was getting my eyes set on my dad on the ground, I tried to run to him but somebody grabbed me and pulled me back. They were standing over him, moving him around and trying to work on him. I was screaming bloody murder.

I knew it was not good. Then I got taken out of the room.

There were so many times that I found him down on the floor or unable to control his body very well. It was the barbiturates.

They held me and took me downstairs. A stretcher went upstairs. I was in the dining room. The front door was wide open. They brought the stretcher down the steps right past me. I didn't see his face, but I saw his head, I saw his body, I saw his pajamas, and I saw his socks at the bottom of the gurney.

I broke free from whoever was holding me, and I ran toward the stretcher. Someone pulled me back. They had to keep working on him.

It was lightning quick.

He wasn't pronounced dead yet. They took him out and I started screaming that I wanted him, that I needed him, and I started kicking and punching whoever was holding me back, trying to get away from them, but they wouldn't let me go.

The front door shut.

To be fair, if I had gotten to him, I would have seen his face, which was distorted, and that would have traumatized me more.

Then we just had to wait. Over and over I said, "Is he

going to be okay, is he going to be okay, is he going to be okay?"

Someone said, "We're just waiting for the hospital to call us to tell us."

I grabbed my friend Amber—she was Ginger's niece—and we went upstairs to my room. I lit up a cigarette while we were waiting, spraying Windex in the air, hoping nobody would smell it.

I remember Ginger had somehow had enough time to do her hair and her makeup. She was dressed to the nines.

It had been about an hour when I heard my grandfather wailing, wailing. That noise. I'll never get past that sound of him wailing. I couldn't work out what he was saying, so I went downstairs.

As I got closer, I could hear, "Ohhhhh, ohhhhh, he's gone, he's gone." Everyone was in the room—my grandfather, Ginger, Aunt Delta, my great-grandmother, everyone.

Everyone but my dad.

"Who's gone?" I said.

"Your daddy's gone, he's gone! My son is gone!" my grandfather said.

I was infuriated. I turned bright red, turned around, and I started to run. Ginger tried to grab the back of my shirt to hold me there, but I just fucking ran. I don't even know where I ran. I think I ran upstairs, back to my room again, and locked the door. I don't remember what I did after that.

I just didn't know what to do. Anger, extreme anger, was my first response; the grief came later. I don't really know why, except that I was angry at the universe that this could happen. I went out on my golf cart, toward one of the trailers in the back. We were watching the news, and then it hit me, hard.

My life as I knew it was completely over.

It's your greatest childhood fear: When you love someone, you don't want to lose them. It's fucking terror and it tortures you. Most kids have that worry. Whenever I told my dad I was scared he was going to die, he'd say, "I'm not going anywhere, I'm not going anywhere."

But he did.

Later, I was walking down the steps in the house and looked at the tour cases. It seemed like he was going to come down the stairs at any moment and they were going to go on tour. Then I remember thinking, *Am I even going to be able to come back to Memphis?*

That afternoon, once they took him away—and this is something I've been upset about my whole life—it turned into a free-for-all. Everybody went to town. Everything was swiped, wiped clean—jewelry, artifacts, personal items—before he was even pronounced dead.

You can still find things from that day coming up at auction.

I heard my mother was coming for me. That was the worst. It felt like an invasion—Graceland was my place with my dad, and I didn't want her there. She was going to wreck the whole vibe. I had my friends, I had people around. Not only was she coming to take me home, which I didn't like, she was also coming to attend the funeral.

Then I had another thought about not being able to come back here anymore. My grandfather was still alive, so I would have an excuse to come.

But would she let me?

She finally showed up and I was on a golf cart with a friend or two. I remember her standing in the doorway at the front steps of Graceland and calling my name, trying to wave me down. I just waved back and kept going. She yelled at me, "How can you be on a golf cart right now?" I wouldn't give her any attention, though—I was so upset.

I didn't understand at all why I got yelled at, but in retrospect, I can understand that she was probably thinking about the fans on the street. They could see me, and she probably thought it would be bad publicity to have me driving around in a golf cart playing with my friends after my dad just passed away.

Because the whole world had stopped.

The viewing was scheduled to be a public event. My dad was brought to the house. They kept him in the living room, the room before the piano room on the right when you walk in the front door. I felt so happy because he was there. I felt lucky.

I sat on the steps that go upstairs with a couple of my friends and watched endless seas of people going through the line and fainting and screaming and crying, grieving so hard. I don't know if anybody saw me, maybe they did, but they were too busy looking at him.

For countless hours I sat and watched.

Ambulances were outside taking people away every hour, people fainting. It felt like the whole country was there. You couldn't even see the streets anymore, there were so many people.

I was so busy looking at everyone else's grief that I couldn't actually have mine yet. I was trying to grieve my dad, but at the same time, I understood he was "Elvis

Presley." I understood his persona and that being Elvis was what he loved doing the most.

Watching other people grieve my father made me not grieve in public. I just didn't. I couldn't.

I don't remember how long the viewing went on, but there was so much drama. I held it all in. I would think, *Wow, look at that person, they're totally losing their shit.* Then I would go grieve in my room where nobody could see me, or at night before I'd go to sleep.

I didn't know what to do with my grief. I would do stuff that would distract me, which would work for a little while, but if I had a minute, I would lose it.

I went down to where he was lying in the casket, just to be with him, to touch his face and hold his hand, to talk to him. I asked him, "Why is this happening? Why are you doing this?"

I knew that soon he wasn't going to be here anymore. I don't remember much after that. I was nine. It was all so fucking beyond me.

It'll hit me still, on and off it comes. There have been nights as an adult when I would just get drunk and listen to his music and sit there and cry.

The grief still comes.

It's still just there.

. . .

After my dad died my world totally changed. Beyond my grandparents, I stayed in touch with Patsy, and one or two people from the Memphis Mafia, like Jerry Schilling. The rest kind of faded away.

My mom stayed in Memphis until everything was finalized and in October my dad was moved from Forest Hill Cemetery to the backyard of Graceland, next to his mother. That was the first time I really felt the loss—obviously from my dad passing away, but more than anything, I felt I was stuck with this woman. It was a one-two punch: He's dead and now I'm stuck with her.

My mom took me to Europe with her sister. Rome, France, and London. She tried to keep me really busy.

They took me to Buckingham Palace. The press was going crazy. They kept finding us wherever we were. But at the palace it was a quiet day. I watched the Changing of the Guard. I was annoyed. I thought, *What are we doing out here? Why aren't we going in? Why are we standing out here trying to get in when people can just come into Graceland?* I didn't understand it.

One night in France I told my mom I was a reincarnated Marie Antoinette and that I had to go to Versailles. So, she took me there and I was walking around saying, "Yeah, I recognize this, I recognize that. . . ."

Before Europe I had been sent off for six weeks to

Rancho Oso, a summer camp in the mountains north of Santa Barbara.

At camp there was a horse I loved, and I rode a lot. That was healing. Then I'd be at the swimming pool, having fun with all the kids, and then instantly not feel right. I would get distracted for a minute and then go, "Oh my God, my dad died." Once I was lying in the sun and an Elvis song came on the radio and I just lay there crying for an hour.

Most of those kids didn't know who I was, and I didn't really care to say who I was, but then some of them started bragging to me that they'd been to Elvis Presley's funeral in Memphis.

"I saw his dead body," someone said.

"No, you didn't," I said.

"Yeah, we were there. . . ."

"I'm his daughter," I said. "You weren't there. I was there. I know."

After camp, my mom wanted me in a good school, so she put me in a ritzy one in Los Angeles. Everyone had a famous father and mother, and I wasn't into that at all.

Then my mom got a French boyfriend and became obsessed with being French, so she put me in a French school and made me do fucking French lessons.

I wanted my other life back.

I always wanted to go to Memphis. I wanted to make sure I could go to Memphis, and that's what she used sometimes to threaten me: "You're not going to be able to go to Memphis if you don't blah, blah, blah . . ." and that would really upset me, but I would do whatever I needed to do. She knew it meant everything to me.

I kept my watch on Memphis time.

She did allow me to go every Christmas, Easter, and summertime. I'd stay with Patsy—who was a mother figure to me—and I would hang out with her and her kids. It meant so much to be part of that family.

Every Sunday was cleaning day, and we'd watch movies, eat biscuits and gravy, biscuits and sausage, drink giant bottles of Pepsi, and go to the video store, or go to Graceland for the night. My aunt still lived there for several years after my dad died. I would go and sleep over there while she was still alive. The kitchen wasn't open yet to the public; I'd stay in the room right off of it.

Upstairs was locked. I could go up there, but I had to come back down. I don't know why, maybe because his room was there. I think there were a lot of conversations going on about what to do with the upstairs to keep it preserved, but Vernon and my mom decided I wasn't allowed back into my room.

. . .

Vernon died in 1979, and then a year later, my great-grandmother died. I remember a car pulling up at school both times. It became a thing that a car would just randomly show up. I got used to it. I started to think, *There's the car, who is it now?*

I had no emotional connection to my grandfather whatsoever. He was a very stern sort of presence. I never got past that with him.

I remember my friend and I messing with my grandfather's face in his coffin when we were in there alone. That's not something I want to say lightly because I know it's truly horrific. There were stitches on him—I didn't understand why then, but I guess they had to open him up and let the body drain.

I was becoming numb to everything. Just another funeral, another loss. Memphis was becoming a place just to go back to for funerals. Enough trauma had happened that it wasn't even affecting me anymore. Everyone was kind of expecting me to be upset, but nothing was fazing me. There was just so much trauma.

Sometimes I'd walk into my mom's bedroom and find her sitting on the floor alone, drunk, listening to her father's music, crying. But she'd never talk about it, or listen to his music sober.

It's difficult to go about your day without hearing an Elvis song out in the world, but I still remember the first time my mom put Elvis on in the car. There were, of course, times his songs would come on in a café or she'd stumble on to them while switching the radio channel, and when this happened, I would catch her leaving it on. But this particular day, when my sisters were little, we were all driving somewhere and I realized that this was the first time she *chose* to put his music on, tuning to Elvis Radio on Sirius as she drove. She told my sisters, "This is your grandfather." I remember thinking it was so strange but also very sweet.

I was twenty-two.

I don't think she ever processed the loss. I think she started to the last year she was alive—she only began using terms like *trauma* as late as 2021. But I certainly knew that she was heartbroken my whole life. I remember when I was little feeling angry at Elvis for leaving my mother and for causing all this pain.

Whenever I would hear Elvis's voice, I would feel my mother's anguish. Feel the loss of him.

My grandfather had known that I'd had a crush on Rory Miller.

After Vernon died, I found out the Millers were moving to Colorado. I was supposed to meet and hang out with Rory before they left—in fact, I'd arranged to spend the whole day with him. Patsy knew it and, last minute, I got a phone call: "Your mom wants you to fly home to L.A. today." Patsy had told my mom, and my mom was not having it.

I was devastated. Rory took me to the airport. That was the first time I remember having actual, real, specific hatred toward my mother.

I saw Rory when I was on tour many years later—I had dinner with him and his wife and Patsy. Rory said, "Your father pulled me aside and told me, you better not do anything, or I'll fucking kill you." My dad didn't use the F-word that loosely, so the message was received loud and clear. Rory said he promised my dad he would never do anything with me romantically, and he promised, too, that he wouldn't ever tell me about the conversation.

"But I think I can probably say it safely now," Rory said.

. . .

My mother sent me away a lot, but I will say that she was really good at birthdays.

One year I remember going to see Queen at the Forum. I'd heard that Freddie Mercury was a huge fan of my dad, so I brought him one of my dad's scarves. I watched the show, and then I went backstage and met Freddie, who was very sweet, very humble, and very moved by the gift.

When I turned ten years old, my mom met John Travolta and arranged for him to meet me for that birthday—he was having a hot moment with *Welcome Back, Kotter*. He talked to her about Scientology, and a few days later, she joined. I was in the car with her and she was describing it to me, saying that it can help you become really powerful. I was always obsessed with *Bewitched* and *I Dream of Jeannie*—I wanted to have superpowers.

Okay, I thought, *that's really cool. I want to do that.*

So now we were members of the Church of Scientology.

My mom would drop me off after school at their building in Hollywood. I felt like she was dumping me there so they could handle me, and she didn't have to. Scientology actually helped. It gave me someplace to go, and somewhere I could be introspective, somewhere to talk about what had happened and some way to deal with it. I took to it quickly and I really liked it.

I got the idea that we weren't just our brains, we weren't just our bodies, we weren't just our emotions. We had those things, but that wasn't all that we were. We were spirits. I would ask myself, "Why are we here? Why am I here? What's the point of everything?" At that point the church felt radical in an exciting way—it didn't feel like an organized religion, really. It attracted cool, unusual, artistic people.

It became my tribe.

At the French school my mom sent me to, all the kids seemed to be celebrity spawns—Tony Curtis's daughters went there, Peter Sellers's daughter, Vidal Sassoon's daughter, Catya. Catya was in my class, and I was obsessed with her because her mother would buy her anything. She always had the newest stuff, like a pair of sandals with heels, which I then had to have. At one point she brought in Liquid Paper and I had to have that, too. My mom was annoyed about it. I remember I wanted to go spend the night at Catya's house—all my friends had gotten to stay over, and she had an elevator in her house! I was so excited to go but my mom wouldn't let me. She thought Catya was spoiled and didn't want me to be around that. My mom would later become friends with Vidal and Beverly Sassoon, and sadly, Catya died of a drug overdose when she was thirty-three.

I can see that my mom had been strong in a good way—more than anything she was worried about me being spoiled. I don't think I was—I think that I could be absent-minded about things, but I don't think that I was deliberately spoiled. I know my dad spoiled me, but my mom did the opposite.

My mom was very strict, in fact. She was never a friend, someone I could talk to.

I felt like I was her trophy. She wanted a cotillion for me. I didn't even know what that was, but she always wanted one. She wanted me to go to finishing school. I felt like she should have gotten a different daughter. It was about how things looked—the way things appeared seemed more important than feelings. My mom would never allow herself to lose control. Everything was all in its place.

My mom was gone a lot. She was on some island eating something she caught out of the ocean, or she was off in some other foreign land, or she was on another adventure with another man, so I started having more nannies and more chefs. She hired lots of people and I became close with many of them.

I felt safest when my aunt and uncle, Michelle and Gary, lived in our house with us. At the time we had a long hallway, my room was near the end of it, and Michelle and Gary's room was all the way at the other end. That hallway would terrify me at night but when they were there, I felt better.

Michelle and Gary were the only two I could really talk to.

When my mom was away, I could have a friend over—that was always my saving grace. But I didn't have an easy time making friends. I still don't. Maybe they thought I was a spoiled brat, when in fact, I was just terrified. There I was in some ritzy posh school with all these celebrity kids and everyone's speaking French and traveling the world and studying like crazy because they want to be the best.

I just wasn't into any of that. I was terribly insecure, frightened, scared, you name it. People wouldn't make friends with me, or they'd get competitive—whose parents were richer, who had the bigger house.

That still happens. And people think that I'm a bitch because unfortunately I have my mom's chilly thing.

I was falling behind in every subject. I would lock myself in my room and listen to my records—music, always, always, always.

Twice a year after he died, I'd dream about my father. The dreams were so real that I would cry when I'd wake up because it felt like I was with him and I hadn't wanted it to end. I'd try so hard to get back to sleep, to be with him again.

I don't really believe they were dreams. I believe they were visitations.

I know a lot of people will disagree with me and think that's nonsense. You might have these kinds of dreams, too, and blow them off and say they're just dreams. That's fine. But I believe that people we love from our past can visit us.

And my dad would do that regularly.

In the dreams, he and I would be together in my room. I'm in my hamburger bed, and he's in the chair. We're close and connected, talking. Suddenly, I get panicked and say, "Wait! You have to stop this, Daddy! You have to wait! You're going to OD, you're going to have a heart attack. Daddy! You're going to die. It's going to happen."

And in the dream, my dad looks at me so calmly, so

knowingly, smiles, and says, "Darlin', it's already happened."

And then I'd wake up.

The dreams only stopped in 1992, when my son was born.

THREE

THE WALL

When I was about ten years old, my mom sent me to a couple of different schools in Los Angeles. One was in Los Feliz, another was in Culver City. Our housekeeper, a wonderful Black lady named Ruby, would take me to school in the morning, and on the way, she would play gospel songs, which were all I wanted to hear because that's what my father had listened to.

The schools were super casual—no uniforms, not rigid like the previous, bougie schools I'd been to—and I found them refreshing. I did well there because I could learn at my own pace. I could just finish an assignment and check it off, done. I didn't have to be anyone special there, either. I felt no pressure at all. I don't do well in groups—work-wise, school-wise, anything-wise—so the individualized learning sang to me. The other kids, too, were really unassuming and normal—there were no clique vibes, no rich kids, no spoiled kids, no bullies, no bitches.

. . .

But still, over the next few years, I started to develop a really bad attitude and I was getting heavily into drugs. They kicked me out of the Culver City school. Scientology didn't want to fully kick me out, though, so they sent me to the Apple Scientology school in Los Feliz. They thought this new school would be more capable of handling me, but I failed everything every fucking time.

I wasn't trying to be bad. I just seriously did not give a fuck. I wore all black, dyed my hair black. I was one of those people with a "fuck you, fuck authority, fuck any system, fuck teachers, fuck parents" attitude. It was around this time I discovered the Pink Floyd album *The Wall*. That record became all I listened to, was all I was interested in. It was my bible and my autobiography.

We don't need no education. . . .

I was always in the ethics office, which was essentially the principal's office. (I can't tell you how many people I've met since who say, "I met you in ethics. . . .") I'd joined that school on probation and never got off of it. I kept either not showing up to something like PE, which I never was a fan of, or not showing up to school at all.

My mom couldn't control me. There was nothing she could do. I was not easy for her. You couldn't torture me to want to learn. I had no interest in being a good kid. So one Friday my mom picked me up from school, drove us up to Montecito where she had a house, and as soon as we got there she said, "Pack your clothes, you're going to school in Ojai."

I knew by then that she'd been thinking of putting me in a boarding school, in Switzerland or on a kibbutz in Israel—I had found four or five applications to different places. I felt like my mom was always actively trying to figure out how to send me away—beyond Switzerland and Israel she had mostly just dumped me off into Scientology because she thought they could handle me. Scientology kind of raised me for her. But every time she'd try to get me into a boarding school, I'd fuck with the admission test and they wouldn't take me.

But now, I was on my way to be a boarder at Happy Valley School in Ojai, and I was mortified. The school was clearly designed for parents who wanted to just send their kids away. For some it was to get a good education, sure, but for others it was just because.

I was there "just because."

The first thing I did when I arrived was look for who had weed. I quickly found most of the kids were of like mind and as spirited as I was, so I started to love it. We were out in the boondocks with nothing to do.

I would stay with my mom in Montecito on the weekends—it was just an hour away—unless I got campused, which meant I had gotten in trouble during the week and couldn't go home. And I kept getting in trouble, so my probation kept getting extended. I would do things like not show up to class, even though we all slept about a hundred feet from where the classrooms were. Sometimes there'd be a drug bust and they'd be investigating who was involved, though it was clearly always me.

I was always falling behind in my studies, lackluster. I'd been terrible at math since birth, just horrible, and I had no interest in a career or even just a subject, anything. I had no interest in being a good kid, either.

As I said, I just seriously did not give a fuck.

I started to cycle through different phases. I was kind of a hippie chick at some point in Ojai, kind of a punk rock chick, a funk rock kid. All I wanted to do was drugs—weed and coke mainly. I wasn't addicted to one particular substance. I liked it all. I wanted to get my hands on anything I could swallow, snort, eat, sniff, you name it. I never ran into heroin, though. Never was in the same room with it, thank God. (That would happen later.) My main purpose in life was just to find a score. I soon settled into a heavy metal phase, dying my hair all black, or bleaching it, and drugs.

But Happy Valley didn't particularly want to throw me out, either, because they knew my home life wasn't so great.

The head of the Apple School would take a group of kids every summer to Spain where she had a house, and even though I was no longer at that school my mom made me go. The five of us kids would take care of the place—gardening, farming—and then have fun at night, hanging out at the beach and partying.

Somehow, I had made it through that first year in Ojai.

When I was young, my mom would drive us to Ojai any chance she got so we could ride horses in the valley. She had a special connection to the Ojai Valley from her time there in school—and she always loved horses, knew how to connect with them, how to recognize when they were scared or irritated. But she didn't want to just trot along. She always wanted to canter and gallop. The horses represented some kind of freedom for her. I don't think she ever realized that her own mother had the same connection to horses.

On the way up to Ojai she'd listen to Michael Martin Murphey's song about the mysterious woman from Yellow Mountain and her pony, "Wildfire"—in fact, she listened to that song on repeat when I was a teenager.

My mom had a few horses in her life she was really connected to. When we lived in Hawaii, she would beg a nearby stable to let her have Misty every time she went to ride—she even wanted to take Misty home to L.A. with her, but the stable refused to let her go.

During the Covid pandemic, she went riding in Ojai all the time. The last horse my mom ever rode was named Corona. She thought that was very funny.

By this point in my life, my mother's role was just to be a chronic stop sign. She didn't try to talk to me, hang out with me, be a friend. I was very much in love with my father's side—they were wildly colorful people and I related to them in ways I couldn't with my mother.

I know she tried her best. She was trying to figure things out and grow up, too, and I gave her a genuinely hard time. I never yelled at her, never mouthed off to her, cursed at her, was never violent around her, anything like that. I was just despondent, extremely melancholy, moody, dark. I'm sure she had no idea what to do with that.

When I got back from Spain I didn't want to go back to Ojai, but I had no choice. I missed the first week, and when I finally got there, some new wild girl had arrived. She had been waiting for me and started following me around. She said, "I've been hearing all about you. . . ." She seemed cool and interesting, but at the time I was having a thing with this German kid, but then she had sex with him, and I thought, *I'm done being up here.* So I pretended I was all strung out on drugs to my mom.

"Mom," I said, "if I stay up here I'm going to die."

Sure enough, she took me out of Happy Valley.

My mom had been dating a guy named Michael Edwards. They dated for about six years in all.

Edwards was an actor and model, a dramatic guy with a horrible temper. He was often on drugs, too. He and my mom would fight constantly, and it was physical. I'd hear her screaming.

They would party a lot, go to discos, and there was a lot of cocaine around. When they'd come home from a night out, that's when I would hear him screaming, the furniture flying. It was so destabilizing.

In the craziest turn of events, Edwards got a part in the movie *Mommie Dearest,* playing Joan Crawford's lover. One day, while he was still making the movie, my mom came into my room, went through my closet, and was yelling at me because I had wire hangers: "Why are you using these? These come from the cleaners! These need to be exchanged for the nice ones, the plastic ones!"

As she was yelling, we could hear laughter from down the hallway.

"The irony!" Michael shouted. "This is too crazy that you're actually yelling at your daughter about wire hangers and I'm in *Mommie Dearest*!"

My mom realized that it was crazy and started laughing, too. I thought, *This is my life now. You're both fucking crazy.*

My mom was going to put me back in the Apple School but I was so far behind in my studies they told her I would need daily tutoring, so I just stayed at my mom's house with Edwards. But of course, I didn't want to be there, either. I didn't really want to be anywhere. I don't know what I wanted.

I probably just wanted my dad.

I was pulling attitude constantly, blasting heavy metal on my record player all day.

One night my mom made dinner, and when I cut into the chicken, it wasn't cooked, so I said so. The next thing I know, Edwards flipped his plate so that it flew across the room and smashed into the wall. I threw my hands up as if to say, "What the fuck?" and at that he jumped up and started screaming gibberish and ran out of the room.

When he got back, he was holding the end of the cord that attached to my record player—he'd cut it off with scissors. He was still yelling.

"Your mother cooks and you just blast your fucking rock and roll, your fucking music, your rock and roll music. . . ." He was making no sense. Eventually he yelled at me to get out. I was in shock. As I left the kitchen, I could hear them start to talk about me, trying to figure out what to do with me.

I went looking for some cocaine. I had some hidden somewhere, but I couldn't remember where it was.

The first time Edwards came into my room in the middle of the night, drunk, kneeling, was years before. I think I was ten. I woke up to find him on his knees next to my bed, running his finger up my leg under the sheets, and if I moved, he stopped—so I moved. I was awake, but I was trying to be asleep.

He said he was going to teach me what was going to happen when I get older. He was putting his hand on my chest and saying a man's going to touch here, then he put his hand between my legs, and he said they're going to touch you here. I think he gently kissed me and then left that night.

I told my mom in the car the next day and I watched her slam her foot down on the gas. At home I ran to my room and she flew into her room and slammed the door. Eventually she called me in and said that Edwards wanted to apologize.

Edwards was sitting on their bed looking very sullen and sulky. He said, "I'm so sorry, but in Europe that's how they teach the kids, so that's what I was doing."

I didn't know what to say. I would always feel bad for him when he apologized.

Eventually it became that he would touch me and spank me, telling me not to look—"Don't look at me," he'd say, "don't turn your head." I assume he was jerking off. He wouldn't be mad at me—he did it very calmly, just sitting in a chair, whacking my ass. My butt would be black, blue, orange, green.

It was kind of the same drill every time. He'd come in the room, do what he did. Once, I showed my mom my butt and she said, "Well, what did you do to cause that?" as if he had just given me a spanking for misbehavior. And then she'd go scream at him. He'd say, "Oh, I was drunk," or, "She was actually flirting with me." And then she would make him come in and apologize. I would feel bad and forgive him.

I was eleven, twelve, thirteen.

He'd still come into my room now and then, but I would move or do something to make him think that I was waking up, then he'd run down the hallway back to my mom's room, freak out, and stay away.

At this point in my life, my mom was trying to have a career. She was trying to be a model and an actress, and she was doing commercials, so she left town quite a bit. And as crazy as this sounds, Edwards was there more than my mother. I was more used to having him around than her.

Every Christmas my mom would give me amazing gifts, but he didn't have much money to do the same, and I would always cry on Christmas Day because I felt so bad for him. He would be really hard on himself, and he played the part of pitiful victim.

But still he had that terrible temper. One morning he made some comment about how I needed to get my panties off the dryer or something. I think I said something nasty back like, "It's not like you're not enjoying that. . . ." under my breath as I was walking out of the room. He took a dining room chair and launched it at me. It hit me in the back—it didn't hit me that hard, but it got me enough to scare the shit out of me. I was crying the whole way to school.

I was crying that whole morning and one of the teachers that I really liked saw me crying and asked me what happened. She took me aside and said, "You *needed* to break down and lose it!" because I was such a toughie most of the time.

There was a lot of violence in the house. I would hear my mom scream and cry, he'd be throwing shit. I wanted to protect her. I didn't know how.

It was really bad on one of his modeling job trips to the Virgin Islands. My mom and I went with him. My mom suspected that he was having an affair with one of the models, and she recruited me to help catch him. At one point my mom went into his room and I could hear them going at each other. I went in there and saw him grab her and throw her on the bed. I launched across the room and jumped on his back, and he threw me on the bed, too. My mom screamed, "Let's go, let's go!" We set off running down the hall, reached an elevator, and hit the button, and he was chasing us while we frantically waited for the elevator door to open, like a scene in a horror movie. Somehow we made it back to my room and he called her—he had turned into a puppy dog again, begging her to go back to him.

When she did, I was so pissed.

The next day I left for Memphis, but I was a fucking mess.

Hearing my mother describe these incidents broke my heart. I know what happened was one of her deepest childhood traumas but I don't think she—or any of us who knew her—fully considered how it may have contributed to some of the fundamental feelings she carried, like shame and self-hatred.

I turned fourteen and my first boyfriend was a kid I went to school with. Initially we were really mean to each other—my friends would say it was because he had a crush on me, and I would get after him, too. But then after one summer when we got back to school, he had suddenly become handsome and his voice was lower—he was not the little chubby annoying prick anymore. So we dated for a year and we did everything but have sex. He was a good kid, but he had a terrible temper.

My mom was doing an acting job, a movie of the week with Michael Landon, in the Bahamas. I went to visit her, and there was this twenty-three-year-old guy who had a small part in the movie, too. I didn't meet him until the day before I left, and I fell hard. We walked on the beach, talking the whole time, and he was really cute. I sat with him while he was packing. I was really sad, then he kissed me, and we left the islands. I remember listening to that song "Torn Between Two Lovers" on the plane ride home over and over and over because I still had my boyfriend back in L.A. who I'd been dating for a year.

When I got home, I broke up with him.

I used to call the twenty-three-year-old and just be silent. So, he got used to this silent caller. He didn't know it was me—there was no caller ID or anything then. The first time he said, "Hello, who is this, hello, hello?" annoyed. Next time he said, "It's you again." Then finally I was punching the numbers to answer yes or no to his questions. "Have we met?" *Beep.* "Do we know each other?" *Boop.* Then he figured it out. I was so nerve-wracked.

The guy was, understandably, horribly apprehensive about seeing me and I didn't know how I was going to pull off actually meeting up with him. One day at school I told my teachers that I had to go to the dentist, and he picked me up a block or two away.

We walked around Beverly Hills all day. I didn't care what we were doing, I didn't care where we were, I didn't care about anything. I just wanted to be with him.

He gave me his ring at the end of it. Then he dropped me off right before I was due back to school.

I was gone. Really, really gone.

My mom found out and I was grounded, banned from speaking to him or contacting him, which, of course, didn't work. Not that I wouldn't have done the same thing if I was her, believe me, but I was not going to be stopped. I was completely, madly in love.

After that there was a lot of sneaking around with him. At some point my mom said I could see him, but we weren't supposed to be alone. We would have to be somewhere my mom knew about and could see. He could come over and hang out or I could invite him to go somewhere that my mom was also going to be, and he became friends with Edwards, of course. He was a twenty-three-year-old being chaperoned by someone's mom. But it was also history repeating itself. My mom was fourteen when she met my dad. I was replaying her life in a weird way, but she and my dad waited until she was eighteen to have sex. I was fourteen when I lost my virginity to this guy.

When I saw him, all I wanted to do was have sex or make out. It's all I could think about. We would find a place to go or be in his car in a parking lot. I'd tell my mom that I'd meet her somewhere, that we were going to just walk around, and then we'd find somewhere to go and make out.

But he was a total womanizer. He'd been with everybody. He was that guy in high school, that guy on the set, that guy. Women of all ages were in love with this motherfucker. And it was so easy for him to keep up his regular life, his other women, because I couldn't see him that often and even when I could, it was only for a short time.

When I met people later who knew him, who went to school with him, they would tell me about a van he had that girls would go into every break, lunch, whatever recess they had. He was a complete and utter player.

And even more, every woman was in love with him. It was crazy. My mother knew a woman at the time who was a *Playboy* bunny. When I started dating this guy, the *Playboy* bunny was already having an affair with him, and my mom told me that this woman was trying to get my mother to send me off to that kibbutz in Israel to get me out of the way.

I was with him for two and a half years.

The ending was just a nightmare.

He took me to a park and had his friend secretly take

pictures of us. They sold the story, got paid for the photos. He didn't care about me. It was just an opportunity to him. Ours was an illegal relationship and selling those photos outed him, but the media at that time didn't care that I was underage and just advertised this personal information.

I didn't know he'd set up the photo shoot. He later denied it, but my mom told me it was him.

When I found out, I swallowed twenty Valium, but I also made sure that somebody saw me. I wasn't that serious about my suicide attempt. I went to the local hospital, and they gave me ipecac to make me throw up and that was the end of that. But I was really devastated. That was my first big love and first big betrayal.

I wasn't going to be happy until I got some revenge. My mom came up with a plan. She didn't want to tell me the details because I was still kind of talking to the guy sometimes. But he was dealing blow, I think, so it was arranged that there would be a drug bust by some off-duty cops. She wanted him humiliated in the process.

She told me they did an anal probe.

The first time my mom told me about this betrayal she said it was her first memory of feeling used, the first time she realized people had an agenda with her. She talked about it regularly throughout her life; it was a core trauma for her. It was just one of a series of events from her childhood that came together to build a foundation of distrust in people—a distrust that she never really got past.

I went back to school, but as soon as they put an algebra book in front of me, I was out of there. I didn't understand why I was there in the first place. No one asked me what I was interested in. If you're going to put a kid in school for all those years, at least find out what the kid's interested in. No one ever told me why I was even in school.

I remember reading my report cards, and from the time I was little all they ever said was that I was really, really tired and that I hated PE. And that I was forlorn.

Actually, everyone who saw me after I was nine, after my dad died, said that I looked so sad.

My mom made me live with her again—but again I was miserable, so I was a terror. It was clear she didn't want me there. She tried to make me go to other boarding schools, but it never worked out, so in the middle of the night she made me pack my bags and she took me to the Scientology Celebrity Centre and dropped me off.

The woman who ran the place took me to a tiny room on the third floor. I was just glad to be out of my mom's house.

The first morning I removed the large mirror from the wall, called my coke dealer, and invited him and about six or seven other people over. We proceeded to have a four-day bender in that room.

I woke up at one point and everyone was asleep. I had a moment where I was just done. I yelled, "Everyone wake up, get the fuck out, out, get out!" I took all the rest of the blow and flushed it down the toilet.

I went down to where they audit people, and I was shaking, sweating, crying. "Help me," I said, though I could barely speak.

They moved me to a really nice room on the sixth floor—it was a luxury palace with a kitchen and a dining room and everything. They made me promise to behave myself and study, create, actually do shit. For some reason, it worked. For the next few months, I actually started to do really well. Then my mother tried to make me move back into her house. And that's when fucking DEFCON 3 started.

It was Christmas.

For whatever reason, I had to go with her and Edwards to Pensacola, Florida, where his daughter lived. She and I were supposed to stay home, and we pretended we had, but we actually went out. We didn't do any drugs, I think maybe we tried to drink, but the point was that I had lied. My mom and Edwards showed up at her house. I saw my mother get out of the car and I took off running down the street with my mother chasing me.

I'm flying, my mom is screaming at me, but she can't catch me. In the end I got in her car—she's in the front seat, I'm in the back, and she's screaming at me because I'm dodging her attempts to hit me. Edwards was trying to get her off of me. I'm punching myself in the face, trying to make it look really dramatic so it would seem like she did it.

The next day we flew back to L.A., and she would not let me out of her sight. During the layover I was trying desperately to get to a phone to call the Celebrity Centre for help. But my mom wouldn't even let me go to the bathroom without her.

Back in L.A., my mom was walking me through the lobby of the Celebrity Centre to go get some of my stuff from my room, and it felt like somebody had a gun to my back. As we walked, I looked at some guy I kind of knew—I'll never forget that he had a black leather jacket, boxers, and black boots—and my eyes got big, and I tried to mouth, "Help me."

My mom got me home that night, and heavy negotiations started the next day. She agreed to let me go back to the Celebrity Centre but I would have to go to their Narconon office and enter their rehab.

"Give me a minute," I said. I went and called the father of a friend of mine and asked him what to do. He told me to ask for twenty-four hours to think about it, which I did, and the next day, I told the rehab that I seemed to have three options: live with my mom and Edwards, go to Narconon, or hit the streets.

I told them I chose the third option.

"Hold on, hold on!" they said. The negotiations continued—this time at a nearby Jack in the Box—and I told them I wanted to live back in the room I'd had there, with my freedom, and that I'd do whatever—reading, studying—but that all I cared about was living at the Celebrity Centre in my room. They eventually agreed.

So I went. And soon enough, I was passed out drunk in front of my room.

And then they actually came up with a great idea. They made me take care of somebody who came in legitimately addicted to drugs. They gave me a car so I could drive her around, help her with life. I became really close with that girl, really took her under my wing.

She was a young mom, addicted to heroin. Her husband and kids didn't even know. I really thrived taking care of her, helping somebody else.

So now I essentially had my own apartment in the Celebrity Centre and made a lot of friends there. And I would still occasionally hook up with the older guy who sold the photos of me. I remember he was living with a woman—I don't know if he married her—but one afternoon I met him at their place and we had sex when she was gone.

The guy wanted to meet up with me more, wanted to have more of a relationship with me, but by that point I had met and fallen in love with a guy named Danny Keough.

FOUR

THERE'S A BLUEBIRD IN MY HEART

I had heard a lot about Danny Keough.

He was twenty-one years old when I met him, and I had just turned seventeen. He was in L.A. from Oregon and was the bass player in a band named D'bat—they'd play small gigs around town. They were all really cute and had a following, and all the girls were in love with Danny especially. They were in love with the lead singer, too, a guy named Alex, but Alex was not as cool or as rugged as Danny—and Alex liked himself. A lot. We used to tease Alex because he would constantly be checking his own reflection in the back of spoons.

I heard later that all the guys in D'bat had a crush on me, but I wasn't paying attention. I've always been really stupid about stuff like that. I don't assume, and I had zero self-confidence back then. And as soon as I heard someone was a heartbreaker or a ladies' man or a womanizer, I put my guard up. I was already guarded, but I'd put up an extra layer if I felt like someone was an asshole, especially after what happened with the older boyfriend who sold the photos. I had those defenses, but I could also be really silly, like a schoolgirl.

I was still living at the Celebrity Centre, though I was also transitioning to living back with my mother. I threw a birthday party for myself at the rose garden café out in the back of the center, and that was the first time I was in the same room with Danny. Our first interaction was just a brief drive-by, and I forgot about it. About a week later I had fully moved back into my mom's house, and all those same people from the rose garden party were going to dinner at the Moustache Café on Melrose. Danny was there and he was making these comments that were bugging me—I thought he was arrogant and super confident. I would respond and I could tell I annoyed him. That night we all ended up at a party up in the Hollywood Hills, and when the birthday cake came out, in front of everybody, I smeared some icing on him, and he took some and put it on my cheek, and then he licked it off.

I freaked out.

I thought that it was just healthy, antagonistic banter, but I found out later that he was on a mission. I told him he wasn't boyfriend material, and that made him want to pursue me. And the cockier and less interested he seemed, the more I found myself smitten with him.

I was with a friend who was living with me at my mom's house. She walked out of the party in the Hills ahead of me. I went out to look for her and caught her planting a kiss on Danny. He pushed her away, and I could tell they were having words, but I found myself angry, thinking, *Danny, you're such a pig. You were just in there macking on me, and then I walk out and you're kissing my friend.*

A couple of weeks later, he told me that my friend had totally blindsided him, probably doing it on purpose because she knew I would be coming out to look for her. Danny was mortified.

D'bat dressed in the New Romantic style, with earrings, silk blouses, necklaces, bandannas, feathers. My dad had incredible charisma—everyone talked about him. He was very handsome, rode a bright red Kawasaki GPz550, and all the girls loved him.

And like my mom, he couldn't care less about fame—he was maybe even allergic to it, just like she was.

The first time my dad laid eyes on my mom he was fixing his motorcycle and she was walking across the

Celebrity Centre parking lot with her mother. She was wearing a black leather jacket, and he thought, *Who is that person with such* attitude? Their eyes met as she passed, and he felt she had looked right into him.

My dad was a jazz guy, and he didn't know that Elvis had even *had* a daughter, let alone that this young woman in the black leather jacket was that child.

The next time he saw her was at the Moustache Café. My parents didn't hit it off at first. "So, you think you're hot shit, huh?" my mom said that night, with a nod to his reputation. He just thought she was aloof.

But he thought, too, that this little creature at the end of the table had such power and presence, and it was nothing to do with being the child of Elvis Presley. (In fact, they would have zero conversations about Elvis throughout their relationship—he knew that she felt the loss deeply, but she never mentioned it.) He knew immediately that she didn't feel the need to impress anybody—and he also found her unbelievably physically stunning, plus she had an intensity he was drawn to.

The playful rat-a-tat continued through dinner until he thought, *I kind of like this person*. He says he developed a crush on her because of her unobtainable qualities. My dad says, "She didn't just lay down and agree with stuff. She was really fiery and would hold her own—in a real way, not just being contentious. I liked the verbal sword fighting. When she said I wasn't boyfriend material, that made me want her more."

I was never someone who had a propensity for quick relationships or one-night stands. If I'm into someone, I'm into someone, if I'm not, I'm not. Hot or cold.

After another party a little while later, I drove Danny home to his place—he was renting a room in some weird part of L.A., like Highland Park. His roommate, a twenty-three-year-old woman, was in the Witness Protection Program because she had turned on a major drug dealer in Denver.

I remember going into his room and we were hanging out, talking, and I spent the night there. Nothing happened. We didn't have sex or anything. I just laid with him, and we were sort of making out and talking. I stayed until the wee hours of the morning and then I drove home alone.

My dad remembers that night a bit differently:

"We had some drinks and were wrestling, throwing stuff around, and we knocked an old closet down and broke it. But my roommate couldn't be mean about it because she was in hiding."

After that, Danny and I solidified into a relationship. I was still being really careful. He'd left a trail of broken hearts—he always broke up with the women, and they'd stay in love with him. His longest relationship had been six weeks. He was so young, but I was even younger, so he was still more together than I was. I was trying to turn my life around—seriously buckling down, starting to pull my shit together, coming out of my crazy phase and my early experimentation with drugs. I hadn't been a drug addict. I had just been super curious and would do whatever came along.

It was really just rebellion.

You must have something bigger than the rush drugs give you, bigger than that feeling, bigger than that happiness, bigger than that emptiness. And that's what I was starting to develop. I wanted to know what the fuck I was doing here, I wanted to know about life, I wanted to know about people. I didn't want to fuck around anymore.

But I wasn't just going to get a job and put food on the table and be content.

I needed answers.

I found Danny's confidence and his cockiness attractive. I tend to be attracted to strong alpha males. I probably get that from my dad. My father was very much the alpha, and I'm a total daddy's girl. But even though I'm a really strong female, that doesn't mean that I want to wear the pants or be the shot caller. I don't mind if someone takes that role.

Danny and I lasted about four months initially—it was definitely the longest he'd ever had, but I worried that Danny had a wandering eye. He could be a slippery son of a bitch, hard to keep hold of. I was completely head over heels in love with him, but he got a crush on some Italian girl who didn't speak any English and had hairy armpits. And we were kind of over after that.

But I always felt like I was hanging on to him. After we broke up, I was heartbroken for two years, stuck on him. Stuck and obsessed. I was one of those girls. I didn't want anybody to know it, but I was obsessed with him.

The Italian girl had been a temporary thing, but I was so devastated. You could not mop me up off the floor.

Meanwhile I would date other uninteresting time-passers. One was Brock the Bug Squasher, a guy who would literally get off on dropping potato bugs and watching them splatter—it would actually give him an erection. That was gross, but Brock was also really good-looking, and in AA. I just used the Bug Squasher to piss Danny off. But all the people I dated knew I was actually in love with this guy Danny, that I was still holding the torch for him.

I didn't know what I wanted except that I wanted to be with Danny. And I knew that I *needed* to have children with Danny, too, which is the weirdest, craziest part of it. I felt like I was supposed to have children with him—I somehow knew that we would always be connected, that it would always be okay, that it would never be a bad situation for a child.

Danny moved away from L.A. for a while, and whenever he came back my antennas would be trained on him. I'd see him at parties, and it would destroy me, especially if he showed up with a girl. I couldn't tell what he was thinking about me. It was cat and mouse for a while—I'd show up at a party with a guy, knowing Danny would be there. I was one thousand percent being conniving and manipulative and calculating. I would watch Danny see me with a guy and his whole disposition would change, he'd be visibly bummed, his energy would drop. But I still didn't think he really gave a shit.

⁂

She chased him for two years. There was no shame in her. But he was just afraid of her fame, was running from the phenomenon of her—he knew she would be his destruction. He was not afraid of much when he was younger, but she scared the living shit out of him.

He felt like a minnow in an ocean of sharks. He was just a bass player. This was way too big.

⁂

I showed up at his place one day and we sat on the curb outside and talked. I said, "This is really eating me up, so let's just talk about how we actually feel, no more games." We were honest with each other, and then a couple of weeks later we went on a date . . . to the MTV Video Music Awards.

Danny almost got arrested that night. At one point a guy—a paparazzo it turned out—came charging at us in the dark and Danny reflexively hit him, and the guy fell over one of those sawhorse barriers. We had to give *People* magazine a photo so that the photographer wouldn't press charges. They paid $70,000 for it.

We didn't think being famous was cool. We didn't really hang out with other celebrities. We were low-key and un-extravagant. I had to downplay things for Danny because he was so proud and I didn't want to scare him off. He would work odd jobs painting, roofing, doing construction, and play whatever gigs he got.

I didn't live like a princess, either. My first car was a used Toyota Celica Supra.

Though there was one night in the China Club when I was sitting with my friends in a booth and Rick James jump-landed right next to me. Rick and I had run into each other a couple times before and he just seemed so broken. He'd say, "Ugh, I'm not doing so good," or "I'm trying to quit and I'm trying to get my life together." I had a soft spot for him. I wanted to fix him.

That night Rick was high as fuck, and Danny saw him getting physically too close to me and shook his head at Rick. Something went *boof,* and Rick got up and jumped through the air like a wild animal to attack Danny. Luckily the bouncer saw it and literally grabbed Rick in midair and threw him out of the club.

Around that time, I got myself a job as Jerry Schilling's assistant. By then Jerry was on the board of Elvis Presley Enterprises, and my mom would have me go to the meetings. I didn't know what the fuck I was supposed to be doing so I'd just sit and listen. My mom was at the helm and wanted me to get trained up for when I took over after I turned twenty-five.

One day I made the mistake of sitting at the head of the table at a board meeting. My mom came in and said, "Don't you ever sit in my seat at the head of the table. Who do you think you are? This is my business, I am the one who opened Graceland. You can't just come in and sit there like you're something!"

But funny stuff happened in that short time working for Jerry Schilling, too. He was managing Jerry Lee Lewis then, and Lewis was the worst possible person to try to manage. But Lewis loved me, was always great with me. One day I was flying back from Memphis to L.A., and I happened to sit next to Jerry Lee. When we landed, the office got a message to me in the plane that said, "Don't get off. Don't get his luggage. There are Feds waiting for him at the gate."

Apparently, Jerry Lee had a briefcase—I presume it

was filled with drugs, Demerol probably. So instead of getting the bag, Jerry Lee and I bucked it out of the airport, the two of us running like fugitives.

But I'm not really a phone person—in fact, the worst thing you can do is make me answer the goddamn phone. And I used to have to answer the phone for Jerry Schilling.

He fired me after about six months.

Danny and I stayed together for a year that time. A whole year. I was nineteen. I even pretended to like his hero, bass player Jaco Pastorius, for him, though I wasn't a jazz fan.

And in that year that Danny and I were together, I got pregnant. But it wasn't the first time I got pregnant by him.

The first time I got pregnant I didn't even know it. During the first four months we dated I had ended up in the ER with horrible pains and they had rushed me into surgery. The doctors thought it was my appendix, but when I came around, they told me I'd had an ectopic pregnancy (while they were in there they took my appendix out, too).

I had never gotten pregnant with any other person, which is fascinating because I'd been equally as sloppy, not using birth control or whatever. But with Danny it happened that first time, and then it happened again when we got back together.

That second time, I didn't know what to do, and neither did Danny. I ended up having an abortion. And it was the stupidest thing I've ever done in my whole life. I was devastated. I did it and we both cried. We were both destroyed and not long after that we fell apart and broke up. I couldn't live with myself.

Danny went off to join the band on a cruise ship that traveled through the Caribbean. I went and traveled through Europe on a Eurail Pass for a couple of months. All the while, I could not believe that I had had an abortion. I was so upset with myself.

So I made a plan.

I planned and I plotted and I schemed. I pinpointed exactly when I was ovulating—I even went to Memphis first to hang out with my aunt Patsy and work out how to make it happen. It was a group effort. I had it down to a science—then purposely planned a trip to see Danny on the ship.

We went to the island of Aruba or somewhere for the night.

I remember getting back on the ship hoping I'd fucking done it.

Danny had no idea of my plan. But I didn't really care

anymore what he thought about it. I didn't care if he wanted to be part of it or not. I felt that I had to redeem, to make amends, because I still couldn't believe I had had an abortion. I thought, *I'm going to have this child. There is a child that I need to be having.* I would be talking to the lost child, saying, "I'm so sorry, I can't believe I fucking did that. Please forgive me and stay with me until I get pregnant again."

Then I left Aruba, waited two weeks, did the pregnancy test. Called Danny up.

"I'm pregnant," I said.

Danny knew he had to marry me. I trapped him. I didn't really mean to, but I did.

My mom subsequently told me every detail of timing her ovulation for that moment in Aruba. And she *absolutely* meant to trap my dad.

The day my dad found out that he was going to be a father, he had been rehearsing in the disco room. The ship was swaying back and forth, and he was holding the drummer's cymbal to save it from crashing down.

Off to the right of the disco room there was a greenroom, and someone called from there, "There's a phone call for you, Danny." This was long before cellphones, and calling a ship was super rare—you had to call a relay point to connect to the boat via wideband radio. Or something like that anyway.

When my dad got to the phone (he remembers what the phone looked like, it was white), my mom said, "I'm pregnant," and my dad dropped the handset. He was in shock because he never planned to be married or have kids. But something made him go, *Let's do it.*

So he quickly recovered, picked up the phone, and said simply, "Okay."

My mom wasn't thrilled—to her, Danny was just a really good-looking wild musician with no real job and no real prospects. This wasn't something a parent would want for their kid. She told me I needed somebody more distinguished, more established.

One day at her house, her latest boyfriend (Edwards was out of the picture by then) took Danny down to the tennis court and when they got back, Danny was pale. Nobody knew what the hell that boyfriend really did—he was always busy having meetings, but nobody ever knew what he was meeting about; he was very Machiavellian. That day at the tennis court, the guy had told Danny that I would throw him out when I was done with him, that he would lose all of his dreams and goals because this thing was so much bigger than him, that I didn't care about him or love him.

The boyfriend said that it wasn't love, it was ownership.

There were multiple attempts to get my father away from my mom in order to gain control of her, and the tennis court was the first such attempt.

My mom was all emotion—she could feel her way through anything—but she wasn't cerebral. My father is deeply intelligent, and that threatened people. He was a problem because he made it harder to control her. There were attempts to have me aborted, attempts to have him followed, incriminated, but he always came back swinging (until it nearly killed him to protect her).

While my dad was on tour, the boyfriend hired PIs to investigate my dad's past and told my mom that what they discovered was so terrible and dark that he couldn't even tell her. When my dad got back from the tour, my mom was incredibly distant and cold toward him, and when my dad found out why, he and my mom immediately went to meet with the boyfriend.

"You have my permission to tell Lisa everything you've found out about me," my dad said. But there had been nothing, of course, and the boyfriend mumbled something about "a mistake" before quickly shuffling out of the room.

I was petrified at this point—it felt like me and Danny against everybody. But I stayed pregnant, and we got married at the Celebrity Centre, with just my mom and a minister and a few close friends in attendance.

About six months later we had a big wedding reception at the Bel-Air Country Club. I wore a white dress for my family and friends so everyone could feel a part of it.

I was very pregnant by then.

I was struggling with the baby weight and getting nailed in the press for it. Back then, they called you fat when you were pregnant. I had so many paparazzi following me, so much attention on me being pregnant, I just couldn't bear it. I was being harassed constantly. For the first time I was getting into car chases, driving crazily trying to get rid of them. Just to go to the store.

Danny and I got our first house, a regular house in the Valley. We were preparing to have our baby, but the pressure was probably the worst I'd ever known.

The police helped us get in and out of the hospital. And that was also stressful, trying to deliver a child and having to post security and police officers on the floor, with the paparazzi trying to get in, and the police trying to get us out like when they try to get the president out of a building.

The day I was born, my parents played a trick on the paparazzi who had been camped out at our small house in Tarzana, right on the street. We didn't have any gate security or anything back then. My dad had a friend who lived on Sunny Cove, a little cul-de-sac off Mulholland Drive in the Hollywood Hills. My dad knew the paps were going to follow them to the hospital, so he alerted his friend when my mom went into labor, and they drove up to the end of Sunny Cove, the paparazzi in tow. The friend then brought his car out and blocked the street and my parents made their escape.

My mom and dad had gone to Lamaze classes. They gave them a focal pyramid—it's their go-to move—and you're supposed to put it up where the woman can focus on it.

When she went into labor with me, my mom was screaming in pain but decided not to do the epidural at first. My dad was trying to help, telling her to focus on the pyramid.

"Fuck the pyramid, and fuck you!" she screamed.

My parents named me Riley but couldn't think of a middle name. Priscilla's mother, Ann (aka Nana), suggested I should be named after my dad. My parents had no other ideas, so they left it up to the hospital, and someone there thought Danielle sounded better before Riley, so that's why my government name is Danielle Riley Keough.

Not long after I was born, photographers came into the room and took a picture. There was pressure on my mom to get a photo of me out into the world so that the press would stop following us. The photo was worth three hundred thousand dollars, which in the eighties was an even more gigantic amount of money, the equivalent of almost a million bucks now. It appeared on the cover of *People* magazine with the tagline, *ELVIS'S FIRST GRANDCHILD. HERE SHE IS!*

And then I had a crash course in being a mom.

I was married at twenty, a mother at twenty-one, similar to my own mother.

But when Riley was born, everybody was happy. She was such a special beacon, a unique spirit, a light in this universe. I think I was a vessel, serving another purpose—Riley was mine, but she was for everyone else, too.

I fell in love with being a mom. I realized I had been called to care for something else. Being a mom was everything to me and Riley was the most precious gem. I was going to do whatever I could possibly do to protect her and raise her.

That thing where you either do what your parents did, or you do the exact opposite of what was done to you? I did the opposite.

Danny got into a band called Ten Inch Men and started playing gigs around town. I developed a bit of a crush on the lead singer—the guy had serious lead singer syndrome—and it became an issue in our marriage. Drunk one night, the singer said to me, "You know, if it weren't for Danny, I think you and I'd be perfect together." I told Danny what he'd said—I was always very honest with him. But it was so hard because Danny would be onstage, and I'd be watching the lead singer. It made Danny absolutely crazy, and it broke up the band.

Danny started doing mushrooms, smoking weed, and it was causing huge fights between us because I had become totally anti-drug by that point.

But mostly we had gotten our shit together.

We moved into a house on Mountaingate, above the 405. We were just like a normal married couple. We were having parties and BBQs with my family.

Now here we three are, living above the 405 in Los Angeles. It's 1991.

"Jaco ran away!"

That is my first memory.

My dad is running, my mom is running. I'm in her arms. She's shouting, over and over, "Jaco ran away! Jaco ran away!" as though by saying it, it might not be true. She's very upset. We're running down our street. Usually, I could hear the cars on the 405 freeway down in the canyon, but today all I hear is my mother shouting, "Jaco ran away! Jaco ran away!"

Jaco was our pug. They named him after Jaco Pastorius. My dad once met the legendary Jaco at Stanley Clarke's house, on Stanley's birthday. Jaco had shown up in a late-model Mercedes—he wasn't yet homeless, not yet completely lost to the drugs. He had already made those classic albums with Joni Mitchell and Weather Report. My dad was sixteen then, meeting his idol.

Now he's ten years older and chasing a different Jaco down the street.

We never found Jaco. Maybe a neighbor took him or maybe a coyote. My parents weren't very responsible back then, but they loved me so much. I never doubted that. Ever.

That was what my mom had felt from Elvis. That's what she wanted me to feel.

But the lead singer flirtation was incredibly hard on my dad because his two zones—family and band—had been compromised.

After one tour my dad came back and said that he had slightly hooked up with a set of twins while he'd been away. He didn't have sex with them—he was proud that it was only kissing and sexy dancing—but he told my mom. She threw a dish like a Frisbee across the kitchen at his head.

Many years later, they discussed it in front of me, and this is how it went:

Mom: Two of them? I thought it was one.

Dad: Maybe it's a different incident.

Mom: I didn't know about any twins.

Dad: They weren't twins actually. They were two friends.

Mom: Oh, two *friends* . . .

Pretty soon after we had moved to that house, my parents started to get death threats. There was one guy in particular, a hill guy from the South—my dad said he had no teeth and was seven feet tall—who was writing letters saying he was coming to get me because, apparently, I was his daughter. "I'm going to kill Danny and get my child back," he wrote from the depths of Arkansas. My dad sent me and my mom to Hawaii and sat in our house with a gun in his lap, waiting for him. My parents had private investigators tracking the man when he got to town, but the authorities could only hold him for a few days in L.A. Hence the gun.

Another time, my dad called the cops to report that

there was a guy with a gun outside our house. They came and stomped him to the ground, and then he sued my dad.

After that we lived mostly in gated communities. We had to.

I loved being a mom so much that I wanted another child, and I wanted a boy so badly. My mom had given me advice on how to have a boy or a girl. Basically, she said that boy sperm gets there quicker than girl sperm, but dies off faster, so if you want a boy, you have to have sex just before the start of your ovulation (to get the first sperm only).

So just like when I planned that trip to get pregnant the first time, I was determined to have a boy this time, and I had to plan it, which meant we only had a certain window. We did it three times in one day and then stopped, because I didn't want to risk the female sperm getting in there.

When I got pregnant, we went to Florida and rented a home there. It was a very easy pregnancy. I was working out a lot at the time, so I was in really great shape. I targeted an increase of exactly twenty-six pounds, which is what I needed to have a healthy baby, and sure enough I gained exactly twenty-six pounds, and it was just my belly, nowhere else.

When my water broke, we drove to Tampa and I had my son, Ben, naturally. We lived in Florida for about a year and a half, and things were great—we both were kind of tamed at that point. It felt settled.

But then I started taking vocal lessons.

The more ferocious the weather, the happier my mom became.

When you live in a place like Florida, it feels like once a week there's a tornado warning or a hurricane warning—Mother Nature is strong there. My mom just loved all that extreme weather. Even though she lived in Southern California on and off for most of her life, she hated the climate there. She didn't like sunshine unless she was on a beach in Hawaii. My mom wanted snow and rain and tropical storms . . . just *something*.

The day my brother was born, I was sitting in the waiting room of the Tampa hospital with my dad's brother, Thomas, and his wife, Eve. It was late, dark. The next thing I remember I am in my mom's hospital room—I am tiny compared to the height of the bed. I'm looking up. It's quiet. My mother and father are there, and so is my new brother. I don't quite remember holding Ben, but I remember the essence of just being there, that nighttime newborn feeling filling the room.

I had wanted to sing my whole life, but I just hadn't. I took the lessons just to warm up my voice, but one day I told my teacher to turn around and not look at me.

I said, "Just listen and if I have a shot at this, or if you think that there's anything in me whatsoever that should pursue this, let me know. If not, then we'll act like this never happened."

With that, I sang a verse and a chorus of an Aretha Franklin song, "Baby I Love You."

When the woman turned back around, she seemed genuinely mind-blown. She made her husband and some other people come in, and then she made me do it again. Even though I knew what I was up against, I thought, *Wow. Maybe I can do this. . . .*

I told Danny I wanted him to produce this track for me. I said to him, "I'll either do this and it's going to work out, or it's going to be the biggest embarrassment of my life and we'll just pretend like it didn't happen."

Danny produced "Baby I Love You" at the legendary One on One studio in L.A. (Danny had once had a job there, but he also got fired for not answering the phone—he was too busy playing bass.) I took the recording around to my family. Everybody's jaw dropped—they couldn't believe it was my voice. So Danny and I started writing music together, and I made a demo tape. And then word got out somehow, and that's when Prince, Michael Jackson, everybody started swarming in.

That demo tape changed our lives forever.

FIVE

MIMI

I met Michael Jackson when I was a little girl in Las Vegas. I think I was about six. My dad was performing at the Hilton and the Jackson 5 were playing down the road. Michael remembered that I went backstage and met them. I don't remember it at all.

When I was a teenager—probably fifteen or sixteen—Michael called my mom for her to go meet him for dinner. When I saw the messages that he'd called, I said, "Mom, what the fuck are you doing? Why is Michael Jackson calling you?" I found out later that he was hoping that I'd come with her. He didn't say so directly because he didn't want it to seem weird.

Then a couple of years after that, when I was working for Jerry Schilling and helping manage Jerry Lee Lewis, Michael tried to contact me via a business guy, John Branca, who worked for the Elvis estate but who had also helped Michael acquire the Beatles' catalog. But at the time I was about to marry Danny, so nothing came of it. Michael told me later that when I was on the cover of *People* magazine after Danny and I got married, he was devastated. He thought that he should be with me instead.

I had no idea all this was going on.

The first time meeting Michael that I actually remember was in 1993, right after he did his famous Super Bowl halftime performance and his interview with Oprah. We met through a mutual friend. I had a demo tape out—he said he'd heard it and wanted to meet me. I didn't want to go at first. I didn't want to become someone else's project. Prince had tried it, too, and though I respected what they were doing, I wanted to do my own thing.

But I went anyway.

When Michael arrived, I was shocked that he was alone, and further shocked that he was really subdued and extremely nice. Danny was with me and made everybody leave the room so that Michael and I could talk.

We just clicked. Phone numbers were exchanged, and he'd call me. I was living in Clearwater at the time, really working hard at Scientology, making progress. Back then I wouldn't even take Advil, which is crazy. But Michael would call. We had worked out a signal: If it rang three times and then stopped it was Michael, and you had to clear the fuck out the way for me to get on the phone with him. We'd be on the phone for long periods of time. I just thought that he was lonely and needed a friend. But he was pursuing me.

Eventually he invited me to go to Atlanta to see him and I went with my assistant, who was also Danny's brother's wife. There, I hung out only with Michael. We went to amusement parks. I don't know why Danny let me do it, don't know why he trusted me.

Mistake.

This went on for a few months, and then the molestation accusations hit. Michael disappeared, went into hiding. Nobody could find him. I put the word out that I was there for him if he wanted to talk to me. He called me pretty much every other day. I was one of only a handful of people who he talked to or who knew where he was.

He went to Switzerland for rehab for prescription painkillers, and then ended up back in Los Angeles. That's when the Northridge earthquake happened, and I heard that Michael ran out of his house in his pajamas, jumped into his Jeep, drove to the airport, and took a Gulfstream to Las Vegas because he was terrified of earthquakes.

I thought that was so funny.

He called me from Vegas and invited me to join him again. I went to the Mirage, where he was staying—I took the kids and my sister-in-law again. Michael and I had different rooms, but each night I'd go to his room, and we'd stay up all night, talking like you do when you're first meeting somebody, watching movies like

Jaws, drinking and talking about our childhoods, our lives, how we felt.

Michael had an energy and a presence, and that week he was fully allowing me into his world, into his mind. I knew he didn't do that very much. I don't think he ever did, actually, until we started talking. He knew that I understood him, and we really connected because I didn't judge him. I completely got who he was and why he thought the shit that he thought. We had come from, and were now in, similar circumstances. Everything about our lives was so incredibly abnormal. There was no reason why we *shouldn't* connect.

And as for that meeting as children? He remembered every detail—where I'd sat, what I'd said.

He said, "You remember the white dress?"

I said, "How do you remember the white dress I wore? My God. You *remember*? I don't remember *any* of this. All I remember was being afraid to tell my dad I wanted to go see somebody else's show."

I was only supposed to go to Vegas for two days, but I ended up staying for eight. Nothing happened physically, but the connection was so insanely strong. No one had ever seen that side of him. He wasn't that high-pitched, calculated thing. That was an act.

At one point during the week I was there, Danny flew to Las Vegas and was trying to find us in the Mirage, banging on doors. I told Danny that I was just helping Michael, being his friend, and that he should leave us alone and go home. And that's what he did.

The final night, Michael again invited me to his room. When I arrived, he said, "Don't look at me, I'm really nervous. I want to tell you something," and then he turned out the lights.

And in the darkness Michael said, "I don't know if you've noticed, but I'm completely gone in love with you. I want us to get married and for you to have my children." Then he played me a song about how he felt and when he finished, he said, "You don't have to say anything. I know I've thrown you off, but I really want you. I want to be with you."

I didn't say anything immediately, but eventually I said, "I'm really so flattered, I can't even talk." By then, I felt I was in love with him, too. I had told him that my marriage was in serious trouble.

I was holding it all in, so when I got back to my room in the Mirage, I totally lost it. I remember walking into the closet, leaning up against the wall, and just dropping, staring. I was so infatuated, so shaken. . . . *Oh my fucking God,* I thought, *what just happened?*

I hadn't wanted to tell him that I felt the same way because I had my two kids with me, and first I had to go home and tell my husband. But I was fully in love, too.

The next morning Michael and I flew back to Los Angeles together on a private jet. When we landed, Michael said, "I'll miss you." And then he said he was leaving it to me, whatever I decided to do, and that he would call me.

When I got home, Danny was in bed, asleep. I was all made up. Every time I saw Michael, I had my hair done, wore an outfit, had my nails done—everything was perfect.

The nails were fire-engine red, and she'd tap them impatiently on the glass coffee table. I'd try to mimic her, but I was too little to have nails that would make a noise.

My mom was a nail biter—she'd bite them down almost to the cuticle, then they'd be bloody, and she didn't want Michael to see them. She wanted to be the perfect woman for him—Michael never knew my mom smoked, for example—which, again, was not dissimilar to how her mother had been with her father. But after she and Michael had been together for a while, he finally told her he liked her nails the best when they were natural—he certainly didn't *require* her to be a perfect woman. She couldn't believe that she'd spent thousands of dollars on nails over an entire year, and he preferred the bitten ones.

So there I was, all decked out, even though I hadn't slept all night.

Danny said, "Come and get in bed with me."

"Actually, I can't do that," I said and left the room.

Danny came to find me.

"Let's talk," he said. "What happened?"

"Well," I said, "Michael asked me to leave you and marry him and have children with him."

"What did you say?"

"I said nothing."

"That's it, then," Danny said. "That's it. Forget it."

And then Danny packed his bags, got the dog, and drove out the damn gate.

Gone.

Within a day, Michael was calling. Was I leaving Danny or not? When Michael found out what had happened, he got really excited and sent giant baskets of flowers. I started visiting him in L.A. I was always in such a state, so nervous. I remember sweating a lot.

He told me he was still a virgin. I think he had kissed Tatum O'Neal, and he'd had a thing with Brooke Shields, which hadn't been physical apart from a kiss. He said Madonna had tried to hook up with him once, too, but nothing happened.

I was terrified, because I didn't want to make the wrong move. When he decided to first kiss me, he just did it. He was instigating everything. The physical stuff started happening, which I was shocked at. I had thought that maybe we wouldn't do anything until we got married, but he said, "I'm not waiting!"

I was sitting on my mom's lap in a hotel room in Clearwater, Florida, when she told me she and my dad were getting divorced. I was hysterical, sobbing uncontrollably because I thought it meant that he wasn't my dad anymore.

"No, no, of course he is your dad," my mom said.

That day, Ben found one of her bright red lipsticks

and drew a long line all along the wall. He always loved to play with her makeup, but this time he was going to be in so much trouble.

"I'm going to tell on you," I said, and I did.

I remember hearing Ben being yelled at in the other room and him crying, and I felt so guilty. I carried that guilt, the guilt of being an older sibling, for years.

Ben could always break my heart.

I think Michael got right at my mom's core. She wanted to fix him, and she felt he was misunderstood, a feeling she was very familiar with.

My father was devastated. After the divorce from my mom, he traveled for three months, first around Italy on a boat with his friends and then down to Mexico. He read a recently published poem by Bukowski, "the bluebird," and it brought my mother to mind. At one point he got lost in a jungle while hallucinating from a drink given to him by locals, and he was rescued by a dog named Searchlight. When he came back, he had a tattoo, a black eye, and orange hair. I cried when I saw him because I could feel how much pain he was in. My brother went to his bedroom and grabbed an eraser to try to remove the tattoo.

When we walked into the lawyer's office together, Danny said, "I don't want anything." There had been no prenup, but I said he had to take something, so I forced him to take a little bit of money.

Danny was amazing like that. He never did anything to betray me. He's always, always been there for me. He literally filed divorce papers so that I could go marry Michael.

We were best friends. We shared every single family vacation together. Riley and Ben never saw anything bad between us. We made it really great for them.

We called Michael "Mimi" because my brother couldn't pronounce his name. Michael was larger than life; he reminded her of her father. She told me that no one ever came close to being like her dad apart from Michael.

At first, we had no idea if they were in a romantic relationship or if this was just a friend she was bringing around. (I like to joke that she was always really good at introducing her kids to the various husbands.) With

Mimi, as with others, we would hang out and do activities together long before she would ever tell us that they were in a relationship.

I don't remember the moment that she told me they were getting married, but I do recall he started sleeping over.

When he would come over her whole world would stop. The front gate would buzz, and a voice would say, "MJ is here." The drive from the gate to our house was about six minutes—in that time, my mom would be scurrying around to fix her lips and put her makeup on.

He would come into our kitchen via the back door. Typically, the kitchen counter was covered in piles of NDAs and tabloids that her assistants would lay out for her—*OK!, Star, National Enquirer, Globe*—so my mom could read all the cover stories about herself. But when Michael came to visit, she didn't leave the magazines out or ask him to sign an NDA. He was probably the only exception.

Michael and my mother were quickly a very big deal. When significant things were happening in our lives, things that would make the press go crazy, she would take us out of school—we had to stay home until it blew over a little. Once we were back in school, we had security outside all day. And if I went to a sleepover at a friend's house, security would sit outside all night there, too. My mom was really affected by what people wrote about her. She had no siblings to share the burden, nobody who understood what it truly felt like. In a way she was the princess of America and didn't want to be.

Her reluctance only made the chase more interesting for the press. There were photographers in trees. My dad was always pushing or fighting some paparazzo.

She genuinely tried her whole life to get away from it. And yet she paradoxically fell in love with Michael Jackson.

Once Michael came into our lives, the fame grew exponentially. I don't think anyone fully anticipated the scale of it. My mother certainly didn't. She rarely thought about consequences.

Michael and my mom got married in the Dominican Republic twenty days after her divorce from my father. She told *Playboy* magazine later that she didn't even tell her mom about it until Priscilla called her and said, "There are helicopters flying over my house, driving me crazy. They're saying that you married Michael Jackson."

My mom just said, "Yup, I did."

I was actually so happy.

I've never been that happy again.

We got married in the Dominican Republic on the DL. There were two witnesses.

And then it was just the two of us, alone. We'd run from rented house to rented house. We'd get into so much trouble. Sometimes he'd call for his main security guy to come hang out with us, but we would end up ditching him because we just wanted to be on our own, to the point where we'd wander into dangerous areas that we shouldn't have been in. But we just wanted to be alone, to be normal, anonymous. I'd do his laundry and we'd do errands together and shop. For our honeymoon, we rented a quaint little house in the gay neighborhood of Orlando, and we'd walk around and look at real estate and go to Disney World every other day.

He wasn't doing any drugs at that point. We were up all night, talking sober.

Michael was an amazing conversationalist. He was someone who never wanted to talk about himself, hated it, in fact, so he would always divert. He was super interested in people, and could really lift them up. He would do anything he could to turn a conversation back to you and what you were doing—he'd be deeply fascinated by everything you had to say about what you did. There was an energy there, something about him that was truly remarkable, something that I've never ever seen or felt in my entire life, other than with my dad.

I feel really, really lucky that he let me in.

I fell in love with him because he was normal, just fucking normal. His normal was a side that no one saw. His mom would say, "He *told* you that stuff?" and Janet would say, "I've never heard him talk about anything like that." I wished that he would show that side more. He didn't really talk to his brothers much at that point, and I think they were surprised that our relationship was legit. But they thought it was really cool.

No one had ever seen him with his guard down. I knew that it was rare. With everyone else, he would snap his fingers if somebody brought up anything he didn't like—snap, and you're out. Because he could create his own world. And in that world, everyone had to agree with what he said.

But in our world, I would say what I felt, and he loved that about me because it wasn't aimed at him. I could be real without hiding anything. He knew I was a lioness with my children—with anybody I loved. He'd have me deal with people, be the bad cop. He respected how and what I felt, and he usually agreed with me regarding people around him and the shit that was going on.

Well, he loved that part of me until we started fighting and I aimed my honesty at him, which was at the end.

Michael lived with us at Hidden Hills. Sometimes we'd stay at Neverland, too, but mostly he was at our house. In Hidden Hills, the call of wild coyotes would send me to sleep, but at Neverland I would wake up to a pet giraffe outside my window.

At home they were a regular married couple. They would drive us to school together in the morning, just like a normal family, though sometimes Michael would bring along a chimpanzee.

Before you ask, 'twas not Bubbles.

He would often sing to us. To my mom, he'd sing the Bart Simpson song "Happy Birthday, Lisa." To Ben, he'd sing "Ben," his first ever solo number one hit. And to me he would sing "You Are Not Alone."

One day, Ben was on the oak tree swing, in his diaper—he often only wore his diaper or no clothes at all, and he was going really high. He was shouting, "Look, Mimi! Look, Mimi!" wanting to show Michael how high he was swinging, wanting to impress him. But

Michael was busy playing with me. My brother fell off backward and hit his head on the ground and began to cry. We all ran over to check on him.

The next day he decided to poop under the swing in protest.

After her marriage to Michael, my mother traveled with ten security guards. When we would drive around, people would throw their bodies at our car, smashing into the windows, screaming, trying to grab us. My brother turned to me one time and said excitedly, "They're following us!" I snapped at him, "They're following *Mimi*."

We weren't allowed to go outside without a hat or sunglasses on. I'm not sure what they thought that would achieve, but I remember hearing my mom and Michael laughing so hard one day as I walked into her closet to find her trying on a ridiculous, long red wig. They both had wigs on, all in the vain hope that she and Michael could go into the real world without being recognized.

My mother and Michael were always very sassy with each other. They talked to each other the same way that Delta talked, or Patsy. Both brought with them generational addiction issues and both of their families came up from poverty, too: Vernon had been a sharecropper and carpenter, Joe Jackson a crane operator. And both

Michael and my mother's father knew all too well what it was like to have godlike fame, a fame that seemed to have appeared overnight.

My mom was very comfortable around Michael's family. She loved having dinner at Hayvenhurst with them.

Michael really wanted kids with my mom from the minute they got together, but she never felt certain about it. She didn't have that feeling she'd had with my father. Whether to have children was a fundamental conflict in their marriage from the start. I know that once in a while Michael would say, "If you're not going to have children with me, then I'm going to find somebody who will." He would also say, "Debbie Rowe told me she will have my children."

To which my mom would respond jealously, "Then go fuck Debbie Rowe." All I knew of Debbie was that she was a kind lady who helped me with my ear infections.

When Michael had called me after the allegations, what he told me at the time was that Evan Chandler, the father of one of the accusers, was extorting him, and I think I told Michael to settle it, everyone advised that he settle because it was going to be a fucking nightmare.

As for child molestation, I never saw a goddamn thing like that. I personally would've killed him if I had.

I didn't want to be on the front lines, didn't want to make any kind of headlines. I grew up avoiding it and hating the press. I did the interview with Diane Sawyer in 1995 to protect him. I thought he needed me, and I loved that. It was really nice for me to be able to play the female role for once, where I could take care of my husband.

After that interview, I got sued by Chandler because Michael had signed a confidentiality agreement with him and had been coached to not approach the subject, but I'd never signed anything. So I would go right in and say that the allegations were not true, and that's how I got the lawsuit. It went all the way down to the deposition stage, but I won.

In 1995 Michael released *HIStory*. I was in the studio with him all the time he was making it. When it came time to do the pre-press, it was clear the pressure was on him. I started noticing differences in him.

For about a year they were riding the high of being newly in love, and then things went downhill.

My mother started sensing there was drug use on Michael's part, and she started seeing behaviors that she recognized from her father.

He began to be more secretive around her. She told me that she thought he was protecting his addiction. At the time, my mom was very anti-drug—she would go on to march in the streets of D.C. to protest the use of psychiatric medicine in children. When she started asking more questions about his addiction, it would cause a lot of friction. They began fighting a lot, and he would ice her for days. I know there was a really bad fight—somebody threw a plate of fruit at somebody. They were two big spirits and they both had big tempers.

Paranoia grew in both of them, and they were surrounded by people whispering in their ears.

During the 1994 MTV Video Music Awards, she had no idea he was going to kiss her until right before it happened. Eventually, the thought crept into her mind, *Did he just do that for press?* Was he just another version of her first love who had sold photos from the park? It sparked a fear that maybe he was only around because she was Elvis's daughter, a novelty. She no longer trusted him. She believed Michael no longer trusted her, either, and he felt that she was catching on to his addiction.

Her distrust of the people around her only grew. At some point Michael disappeared for days and my mom couldn't find him. She was reaching out to his circle, but no one would tell her anything.

Michael started going to the doctor's office a lot. I'd pick him up and he would be really out of it. I think it was Demerol shots. He said he needed it because of his scalp injury, but I knew there was a longer story to it, that it was big. One of his family members told me that it was a pill habit.

He was about to do a giant HBO thing, and I think he didn't want to do it, so he feigned a fall and went to the hospital. I kept asking what was wrong with him, and I got a different answer every day. Karen, his makeup artist, told me that he'd totally planned it because he didn't want to do the HBO thing.

I flew to New York where he was in the hospital and was with him every day. His mom was there, too, along with his team, including his own anesthesiologist. Nobody has their own anesthesiologist—every hospital has their own. It was a big red flag. At first, I couldn't get a read on what the fuck was going on, but I started to cotton on to it: He needed somebody around who could legally administer the drugs. I told one of the security team that I wanted to go into his bathroom to see what he was taking. A family member asked me to try to get his urine to test it, but I didn't.

Michael was being really awful—he got mad at me for asking questions. I said, "What's really happening here? If you have a problem, I'll go with you to rehab." The doctor started coming after me, threatening me, telling me to stop asking so many questions. I said, "I'm just trying to find out what's going on with my husband."

The doctor and Michael had a meeting, and when the doctor came out of his room, he said, "He wants to talk to you."

In the room, Michael said, "You're causing too many problems here. They're going to take you to the airport, you need to go home until I'm done. I'll see you when I get back."

So I left. I wanted him to come, too, but he didn't.

I filed for divorce very shortly thereafter.

Somebody had told my mom that Michael was planning on filing for divorce but that it would be better for her if she did it first. My mom told Oprah in 2010 that she made the decision to walk because she saw the drugs and the doctors coming in, and they scared her and put her right back into what she went through with her father.

So, she filed. But the truth was, Michael never intended to file. It was *Romeo and Juliet,* the poison mistakenly drunk. Michael was incredibly hurt, and my mom tried and tried to reach him, calling and writing him. But he refused to speak to her.

My mom always said that was how she learned to ice people, from Michael. Eventually, they started talking again and hanging out. They had a back-and-forth, sort of toxic relationship going on. He told her he was going to marry Debbie because he wanted kids. Their divorce was finalized in August 1996, and Michael married Debbie three months later. But we'd still go to Neverland.

I'm not really sure what the vibe was between my mother and Michael—I don't know if they were still hooking up or not—but we were certainly over there a lot.

We went back and forth for years.

He had wanted me to have his children so badly and I didn't want to. I knew he ultimately wanted to be the only caretaker of the children. Michael wanted to control things. He didn't want a mother influence, or any other influence, in fact.

I figured that Michael would have me have the children and then dump me, get me out of the picture. I could read him like a clock. I understood everything, and I knew everything about him because all we did was bare our souls to one another. I knew his nature, and he was very controlling and calculating.

One time he was working, and he called me. During the conversation I said, "You're like a snake—I don't know what you're going to crawl out from under. . . ."

Michael said, "Oh, that's great. I call home and talk to my wife, and she tells me I'm a snake."

"Well," I said, "yeah, you are."

In 1997, my mom flew us all to South Africa, where we watched Michael perform for the last time. (We'd sit at the side of the stage while he performed, and he would bring me and some other children out onstage during "Heal the World.")

On the way to the show, our private plane had almost gone down—we made an emergency landing in a village in the middle of nowhere. The near disaster felt like a bad omen to my mom.

After South Africa, my mom realized she needed to break off whatever this relationship had become. It wasn't good for her, and she cut Michael out of her life.

Years later, Michael called my mom. She said he didn't sound sober. He said, "You were right. Everybody around me wants to kill me."

It was their last conversation.

My mom was in London, writing a record, when Michael died. My mom later told Oprah that Michael often said he was afraid of ending up like her father. He was forever asking my mom about when Elvis died, how it happened, where, why. Michael said, "I feel like I'm going to end up the same way."

At Michael's funeral, my mother sat with his coffin for hours after everyone left, just like she had with her father. She told Oprah that she didn't think she could make peace, that it was more like she wanted to apologize for not being around.

My mom told me that she communicated with Michael through her dreams for months after he died.

SIX

TEN YEARS

As I mentioned in the preface, when my mother sat for the interviews that form the basis of this book, she wasn't in a place where she could recount all the great, fun times in her life. She focused mostly on the trauma.

Accordingly, there is much less material on the tapes about the years between her divorce from Michael Jackson and her marriage to Michael Lockwood, a gap of about ten years in which she created a magical life for me and my brother and was surrounded by a large group of devoted friends. These years constitute some of the happiest times of her life. But they were also years in which the scale of her life ballooned to almost a breaking point.

Fortunately, my mother told me everything about her life (which, again, could sometimes feel like a curse for me as her daughter, but I was happy she did when I was working on the book). So, much of the material in this chapter is my recollection of what she told me.

. . .

In Florida we lived in an area called Belleair. There was a sort of swampy, Southern feeling to the place, with fireflies and alligators and the trees covered in moss.

We lived in a big, old house. To the right of the front door there is a bedroom, and I am peeking through the door. It is dark in the room—all the shades are down even though it's daytime. I'm watching my mom shushing my brother—he is on her shoulder. I remember the rhythm of it, the *sh-sh-sh,* three notes repeated over and over.

I realize now that this was my first understanding of the depth of her maternal instincts—my mom had the strongest such instincts of anyone I've ever met. Eventually it would be clear to me that should anyone hurt Ben or me, she'd probably track them down for as long as it would take, like in a Western. This was the presence you could feel in her, and it wasn't small. It was terrifying.

Something else that's terrifying: I only have fond memories of Ben, but my mom once told me that shortly after he was born, I said, "I wish all the babies in the world would die." Clearly this was my way of saying I felt upset about this baby.

I had an instinct that Ben was the love of my mom's life.

My brother and I often would talk about how magical our childhoods were. Maybe it was just the time and the place; maybe we were just lucky to find ourselves in some kind of golden moment. What was certain was that we had extraordinary parents who wanted us to have joyful childhoods.

My mom got us a nanny each—I had Idy, who was a teenager, but Ben had Uant, who was from South Africa and in her sixties (her real name was Suzanne, but he couldn't pronounce that). Uant was so great for him—they'd play in the garden all day, watering plants and getting muddy. When Ben learned to talk, he developed a bit of a South African accent from being with Uant all the time.

Ben had curly ringlets down to his butt, and a lot of people thought he was a girl. He loved being in nature, a little nature boy, and he was sweet, soft, and gentle, an old soul.

Just as Elvis had with his mother, and my mom had with Elvis, my brother and my mom had a kind of "I can't live without you" relationship. They shared a very deep soul bond.

Ben was very similar to his grandfather, very, very, very, and in every way—he even looked like him. Ben was so much like him it scared me. I didn't want to tell him because I thought it was too much to put on a kid.

We were very close—he'd tell me everything. Ben and I had the same relationship that my father and his mother had. It was a generational fucking cycle.

Gladys loved my dad so much that she drank herself to death worrying about him. And then my dad had his demons and acted out on them. I have everything in me that wants to do the same thing. And then my son's got the same genetic makeup—I feel like he's more genetically me than Danny.

Ben didn't stand a fucking chance.

When I was about seven years old we moved to a new house a bit farther north in Clearwater, on Osceola Avenue—our dock was on the ocean. Ben and I would jump off that dock into the mud when the tide was out, rolling our whole bodies in it, covering ourselves in this disgusting ocean ooze, playing with the seaweed and the dead fish and the shells. Some days we'd go find lizards, and we figured out that if you pushed on the belly of one it would open its mouth, and when you let go it would snap shut—that's how Ben could wear them as earrings. In our backyard we had a pool, and at some point every day, my mom would yell from the house to get out when the thunder and lightning came, though we'd always try to stay in the water—it was more fun when it was raining and when the sky lit up.

My mother's favorite thing to do was take us to the park by the lake to go on the swings. (*She* liked going on the swings, not pushing us on them.) Her two rules in Florida, which we'd hear often, were you can't swim in the rain, and if an alligator chases you, you have to run in zigzags.

My mom would take us out into Clearwater Harbor on Jet Skis, doing donuts and throwing everyone off the back. It was that same energy she'd had at Graceland with the golf carts—totally wild. She once threw her mom off the back, then freaked my grandmother out by pretending there were sharks coming for her.

Other times we'd head across the harbor to a tiny

island covered in sand dollars. We'd collect them, bring them home, dry them out, and then crack the Aristotle's lantern open to find these little dove-like shapes, which were actually their teeth, poor things.

I still feel bad for the lizards and the sand dollars. And my grandmother.

My mom would take me to the Sandcastle to get frozen yogurt in a cone, just me and her. She would have the music blaring in her black Mercedes—always a black Mercedes—and we listened to Toad the Wet Sprocket (it was the nineties) and Toni Braxton and Mark Morrison's "Return of the Mack," though my mom loved all R & B. My mom would always sing along in the car, but in a self-conscious way, as though she didn't want anyone to hear her. I didn't understand back then why she was scared about music.

After the divorce from Michael, my mom started having panic attacks. This is why she took us out of L.A. and to Florida to begin with. They were so severe that she was in and out of the hospital. Even in Florida she had to put aluminum foil over the windows so the paparazzi couldn't take photos of her. She had her gallbladder removed and the mercury taken out of her teeth. But nothing helped because it wasn't just physical. She was having a sort of mental breakdown.

Just as my mother used to pick up the phone to listen in on conversations between Elvis and Ginger Alden, I once unwittingly picked up the phone in Florida in time to hear my father—who had just seen a photo in the press of Michael Jackson, my mother, me, and Ben—say, "Get my son off that guy's fucking lap." I quickly hung up the phone. Strangely, this was the first time I realized my father was upset about my mom's marriage to Michael—that's how well they protected us from their adult problems.

Despite his hurt, my father recognized that my mom needed help and flew to Florida to look after all of us.

She told me later that that was the last time they hooked up.

My mom desperately wanted to get back together with my dad. She believed she'd broken up her family and felt immense guilt, but my dad couldn't risk being that vulnerable again.

At night, my dad and his friends would sit on the balcony of our house and play and sing while the tropical storms came through. One night my mom and my dad and all of us sang "Leaving on a Jet Plane" together, while the weather raged. Both my parents loved rain and hated the sun—they had chosen my brother's middle name, Storm, during Tropical Storm Earl.

I really had no prototype to follow growing up. I had no family life, no home life to be an example, ever. No stability. I didn't feel any emotional attachment to my grandparents, who seemed to be perfect, who did all the right things and made all the right moves, who got married and had kids and stayed married until they died.

I guess I didn't really have a shot in hell.

If something is not interesting to me anymore, I'm out of there. And whenever you get with a new person, the whole thing—the beginning, middle, and the end—will play out in two years. That's why I got married multiple times.

When I had Riley, I set my mind solely on having a child and raising a child. Was my goal for her to have suitable parents who were stable, and were Danny and I going to stay married forever? No fucking way. Neither of us had that in our minds. But we were a different kind

of soulmates, and always ended up living in the same house somehow.

My parents began to record music in my mom's garage in Florida. These would become some of the songs on her very first record. They would write during the day and at night we'd all go get frozen yogurt or go to a movie theater to see something (my mom always got a medium popcorn and a red Icee).

She was usually very protective of us, making sure we didn't see anything too grown up—I remember seeing *Flubber* at the local theater, but I also remember being dragged to see *Titanic.* She kept her hands over my eyes during the entire sex scene in the car. So I was allowed to see the catastrophe of the sinking ship but not the boobs. She inherited the modesty from my grandmother.

Some days she'd take us to the Dairy Kurl in Clearwater to get chocolate-dipped ice cream cones.

While our parents were recording in the garage, Ben and I would ride our bikes around the front yard. Every afternoon around three our neighbor would come out on the porch of his old Victorian house, sit on a chair facing the ocean, and play the fiddle. Me and my brother would climb our kumquat tree so we could see over the high walls. And there we'd sit, eating kumquats, watching the man play.

Once he finished, we'd climb back down and head out to the front yard and the ocean to search for manatees, but we never found any.

Once my mom fully recovered, we all moved back to California, back to the house we had left behind.

Our house in Hidden Hills, about thirty miles west of downtown L.A., would turn into our real childhood home. My father had found it for us. We lived there till I was twenty-one. It was a very special place, though it has since been torn down. There weren't a lot of celebrities around there back then. It was a horse community, and everybody had one. My mom liked that it was far away. She liked that no celebrities lived there.

We had five acres. There was a swing out front on a huge old oak tree, fruit tree groves in the back, the main house, another full-sized house, and two guesthouses. I remember going to see the house for the very first time—when I laid eyes on the swing on the six-hundred-year-old oak tree, I was sold.

The main house at Hidden Hills was rustic, with stone fireplaces and wood beams. Snakes would get into the house sometimes, and at night we'd hear the coyotes howling, great horned owls hooting. Sometimes I'd turn a bathtub faucet on and spiders would come out. We'd often find tarantulas in our backyard. I would bring them to school in jars as my show-and-tell.

My mom's assistant and her son lived with us—he was our godbrother, and he and Ben and I would just roam. We were crashing bikes and running off finding snakes and getting cuts and falling into rosebushes, running amok like my mom had done at Graceland. I think we were protected by angels because none of us ever broke a bone, even when we fell off swings or crashed golf carts. Once, my brother flipped his golf cart—his had off-roading tires—and decapitated it. Somehow, he was fine.

Along with the horses and seven dogs, we raised goats and chickens and peacocks. Ben and I would spend hours, sunup to sundown, playing in those orchards behind the house. We would imagine ourselves into worlds we created, constantly coming up with games and spending hours in the trees playing make-believe.

We would climb in the apple trees and the plum trees and the pomegranate trees, until we cracked open a pomegranate and ate the soft insides. My brother's nanny, Uant, would ring a bell at four o'clock for tea—tea and crumpets and jam, like some colonial British version of her South African upbringing. My mom curated all that for us—it was her version of Graceland.

The decade after Michael Jackson was her best time outside of the Tarzana days with my dad, when things were simple. She had so many friends who really loved her. We would joyously travel the world together as a pack of twenty-five people. Fun every day, all day. I'd wake up to find a whole bunch of people on the deck drinking coffee. It was a dreamlike communal life. We were never alone. She was never alone.

Because my mother had been a witness to Michael's life, we now had a private chef, three assistants, ten security guards, agents, business managers, friends, so many people coming and going. At all times all of the houses on the property were full. Three of my friends moved in with me in the main house, and we even had my mom's holistic doctor living upstairs, plus the two nannies, so in all about seventeen people could be living there, and then there were the people who would come by every day. She wrote a song, "Thanx," about those friends on her 2005 album, *Now What*:

> One day
> On one tombstone
> All our names should go
> We shared a life
>
> The beauty
> And the ugliness
> Through all the pain and death
> The birth of a child.

My mother had a Gaia-like quality, a mystical intuition. Sometimes it felt like Mother Nature lived through her.

One morning, my mom and dad were sitting in the kitchen drinking coffee when two of her friends, Mike and Caroline (who she had set up and who were now married and lived with us in the upper house), walked in.

"You're pregnant," my mother said to Caroline.

Mike and Caroline went white. Caroline was indeed pregnant, but only a few weeks. And they hadn't told anyone.

As early as ten years old I was talking about past lives—I felt like I'd lived them, could remember them at one point, but I can't remember them anymore. I wish I could. I think that we've lived before, and I feel like the things I remember have something to do with how I died in some other lifetime.

I remember when I was young, telling people I was on a horse and buggy or in a carriage at a time when there were no cars. They always thought I was crazy when I said that, but I didn't raise my own kids to think those kinds of things are crazy. My kids would say the wildest shit as early as three years old, and I'd just say, "Really? That's cool!" I never wanted to say, "That doesn't happen," or "That's not possible," or "You don't know that." I never felt like I had to cut them down like I was when I was young.

Both my parents wanted the world to feel magical to us.

My mother would hire a Santa Claus to run through our yard on Christmas Eve, my dad would take us fairy hunting in the forest. My mother's bathroom had a secret little garden attached to it. I always thought it looked like a fairy garden, and I told Ben that's what it was. "If you ask the fairies for presents," I said, "they'll bring them." At the time he loved to play with my Polly Pocket dolls, and whenever we went into my mom's secret, magical garden, he'd ask for a Polly Pocket. One day I went to the toy store and got him some, and tied them to the trees overnight. The next day he ran in there and I said, "Look what the fairies brought you!"

As I got older, I entered that phase where a younger brother is a burden. I was around eleven when I got my first AOL account, and I'd rush up to my mom's computer and hope I'd gotten an email. One day Ben joined me and said, "I have a magical potion for you to drink."

This was annoying for an eleven-year-old girl hoping to get an email.

"Go away! I'm busy on my email!"

"But it's a magical potion," he said.

"No, it's not."

"Yes, it is—it's going to make you fly!"

"No, Ben, it's not going to make me fly," I said, though I did still secretly believe I could fly.

I was killing the magic, and I knew it, and he was so sweet, so I said, "Okay, I'll try your magic potion, but it's not going to make me fly. Watch . . ."

I took a gulp of it and immediately regretted it.

Despite having a mouthful of foul liquid, I managed to ask, "What is in my mouth?"

"It's my pee," he said.

Then I was, indeed, flying, just like Ben said I would, down the stairs and the long hallway all the way to my bathroom. Ben followed me and stood laughing at the doorway as I spat out his magical potion and brushed my teeth with soap over and over again.

I went and found my mom.

"Ben made me drink his pee!" I wailed.

"Benjamin . . ." she said, and that was it. He never really got in trouble. All he would ever get was "Benjamin . . ." And if he was really in trouble, "Benjamin *Storm* . . ."

Everyone loved him too much to stay mad at him.

Another time I chased him into the laundry room, telling him I didn't want to play with him because he was being such an annoying little brother. I remember I had a VHS cassette in my hand and I was so angry that I lifted it up high like I was going to hit him with it. He started sobbing.

I have felt bad about that for my whole life. Like I said, he could just break my heart so easily.

Because he was the sweetest little boy you could imagine.

. . .

We went to a private school in Woodland Hills called Lewis Carroll, three stop signs down the road from our house. My mom would pick us up at the end of the day, but she didn't really have a lot of interest in our education. We didn't have to be sick—we could just tell her we didn't want to go to school, and she'd say, "Great! You're staying home and hanging out with me." Even on the way to school sometimes, Ben and I would pitch to her all the reasons why we needed to stay home that day, and as we'd be pulling up to school, she'd turn the car right around and pull back out, and we'd end up getting ice cream or going to the toy store.

My dad, on the other hand, said we needed an education, a schedule, structure. But my mom ruled the roost, and if she wanted something, that was the way it was. My mom let my father homeschool us at one point. All I remember is him telling us about ancient Egypt. How Orion's Belt aligned with the great pyramids. To this day, I actually impress people more often with my knowledge of constellations than with my math.

. . .

A couple of years before I was born, Priscilla had a second child, a boy named Navarone. Priscilla was a new mom again, and my mom was a new mom, so they spent a lot of time together because they both had little kids. It became a point of understanding between them, a new start, a burying of the hatchet—though I know my mom was a bit jealous of Navarone, too, because here was this little boy that Priscilla just adored.

Nana, Priscilla's mother, was the matriarch of our family, and the quintessential grandmother. Whereas Nona (Priscilla) didn't really fit the image of a "granny," Nana definitely did. The entire extended family would have dinner at Nana's house in Brentwood every Sunday. She made famous burnt baked potatoes, and we would all put our salad in the potato skins and eat them. Sometimes she'd make us pasta and we'd eat it with cottage cheese. In fact, my mom would never eat pasta without cottage cheese—she said it was a "Beaulieu thing," referring to Priscilla's maiden name. After dinner my grandmother would always have Push Pops for all the kids.

I felt lucky we had such a big family and so many cousins. I had loads of cousins—maybe twenty in all—and we had the best time for so many years, so much fun and joy, so many trips to Hawaii—a normal family, if famous.

We'd spend most Thanksgivings at Nana's, and we would often go up to her house in Lake Arrowhead around the holidays, where we would run wild outside, climbing on boulders and looking for arrowheads, while the adults drank wine and watched movies.

Nona would regularly pick me up or my mom would drop me at her house. I probably saw Nona once a week at least. Every holiday, every Christmas, every Sunday, we all spent them together. I was dimly aware that my mom and her mom had had real issues when my mother was younger, but if you look at family photo albums or home videos, you'd see a very close family.

Later, in our teen years, Navarone and I went to the same school, so often I would sleep over at my grandma's so that we could drive to and from school together—he and I became close.

I wasn't aware of the full details of my mother's relationship with her mother until much later. For a long time, they let the past be the past so that Priscilla could be a grandmother for us kids. From my point of view, we were a close, normal family. Those Sunday dinners at Nona's went on well into my twenties.

There were a solid two decades where our family felt very normal to me.

. . .

My mom took me everywhere with her when I was a kid.

I remember she did a photo shoot in New York with Kevyn Aucoin. He made her up to look like Marilyn Monroe—I couldn't believe how beautiful she was and how much she looked like her. Once he was done with my mom, Kevyn did my makeup, too—I vividly remember his deep voice and his big hands. She would take me to Cartier photo shoots, *Vogue* photo shoots, and once to a fitting with Donatella Versace. While my mom was trying on dresses I ran around the studio with Donatella's daughter, Allegra. When we left that day, my mom took with her an extraordinary, very heavy, sequined Versace dress. I'm not sure how often she wore it but I loved to visit it in her closet. It was magical to me.

One of my favorite things to do was sneak into my mom's massive closet when she wasn't home and try on her dresses. She hated it when I took her things. One day, when I was thirteen, I snuck in and borrowed one of her favorite bags, a black Chanel purse with a gold diamond eagle on it. I was going to Six Flags with my friends, and I thought it would be cool to take the purse. But on a break between roller coasters, I put the bag on the bench behind me, and when I stood up to leave it was gone.

That was the only secret I ever kept from my mom

when I was growing up. Eventually, when I was about twenty, I told her. I don't think she could even remember which Chanel purse it was, she had so many.

I would often find myself at parties with her. When I was around nine years old my mom took me to a party at Alanis Morissette's house on the beach in Malibu. My mom didn't really know anyone at the party—she didn't go out of her way to make friends because she was really shy by nature—so I was her friend for the night, which was common.

At some point we got some vegan food—I remember there was a lot of vegan food—and for the rest of the night we sat alone by a bonfire on the beach chatting. Through the darkness we realized there were two adults rolling around on the sand making out. My mom covered my eyes.

"Don't look," she said.

When my mom would go to parties in the Hollywood Hills, if there was a person there who she thought I was a fan of and would want to meet, she would call me to get out of bed in the middle of the night to come to wherever she was.

One night after I had fully gone to bed, somebody came in with a phone for me.

"I'm at a party," my mom said, "and you'll never believe who's here!"

"Who?" I said groggily.

"Marilyn Manson! Do you want to come meet him?"

At the time I was a big Manson fan. So even though it was a school night and an hour's drive from Hidden Hills to the Hollywood Hills, security took me to the party at Jacqui Getty's house. I met Marilyn Manson, and then went upstairs where there were some other kids. We tried on wigs all night until the adults were done.

Much later, on my seventeenth birthday, when I was deep in a Led Zeppelin phase and had gotten a ZoSo tattoo, my mom called me from Peppone in Brentwood. "Let's have dinner for your birthday!" she said. Again, security drove me over. I met my mom in the parking lot, we walked into the restaurant, and there was Robert Plant waiting to have dinner with us.

Most nights I would fall asleep to the sound of a party, the piano being played and people singing, the music loud. Ben and I would sometimes sleep together in the same bed, that was very comforting to us. My mother had other boyfriends, but my dad still lived in the guesthouse.

My mom's routine was the same every single night she was at home: a massage while she watched *Nick at Nite*. Then she would come and lie with us and sing us a lullaby—*Mama's little baby loves shortnin', shortnin'. . . .* or *Lullaby and good night, Mommy loves you, Daddy loves you.* That's usually where that song ends, but she would keep going, naming every single person and animal we'd ever met, until we fell asleep: *"Grandma Janet loves you, Nona loves you, Idy and Uant love you, all the dogs—Oswald, Ruckus, Lulu, Winston, Puffy love you. . . ."*

Or my dad would read us *The Hobbit*. Then they'd both say good night, some nights a bit tipsy and wild, in which case our nannies would sit with us until the sound of coyotes called me into a dream I always had, a place in which nothing bad ever happened, and where we all lived forever in each other's orbits, the closest family you could imagine.

Holidays were a huge deal for my mother. Christmas morning we'd find puppies crawling out of stockings. At Easter we'd get baby chicks and bunnies.

For her birthdays, she would rent out part of Magic Mountain like her dad had done with Libertyland in

Memphis. She loved roller coasters. Zippin Pippin was the first roller coaster she ever fell in love with, so on one birthday she just rented out Colossus and went on it about seven hundred times in a row all night with me and Ben. She made her security guards ride with her until they turned green.

We'd have huge Thanksgiving meals with everyone dressed up. Nothing was low-key. She wanted every moment to be extraordinary.

But then there were those nights when I would come in her room and find her alone, lying on the floor listening to her dad's music, crying.

It was hard for my mom to have a music career. She was a beautiful lyricist, but she didn't feel like she had real control over her music. I thought it was so brave for her to make a record at all.

After a day in a studio, she'd call me and my brother to go sit in her Mercedes and listen to the song she had recorded that day. She'd play it for us very loud, and then we would tell her what we thought. And if we weren't at school because we ditched out, or it was the weekend, we'd go with her to the studio—there was even a song that she wrote, "So Lovely," about us, that we got to sing on:

You know I did something right
Something that keeps me alive
Oh you sweet little babies
When you came you let me know why
I was finally happy
You knew me before now didn't you
My God you're so lovely
Did you come here to help me
And I know you can't sleep well
Unless I'm right there next to you
Oh you, you take care of Mommy too
You're so quick to defend me aren't you . . .
Please don't fear to lose me
You know I have those same fears too

My mom loved touring, but it wasn't lucrative for her because she wasn't giving people what they thought they wanted, which was for her to cover Elvis songs. Elvis impersonators would come to her shows. She always dreaded that. She would peek out the side of the curtain before every show to see if any impersonators were in the audience to prepare herself. How weird to have someone wearing a costume of your dead father watch you sing. She really wanted to be taken seriously, but it was kind of never going to happen.

Despite the Elvis impersonators, my mom loved the

tour life. We loved it, too—we'd go on the tour bus with her, sleeping in bunks, going from city to city, in and out of motels to shower and then on to another town, another Cracker Barrel and another Waffle House, sound check, take a nap, play the show. She loved finding local bars and playing and then hanging out. Sometimes she'd invite fans to come back and party with us in the greenroom after a show.

I loved performing live, loved the instant feedback, the give-and-take with the audience. In the studio you're often in the room by yourself, but live, I could watch people's faces and see how my words or my music affected them. I could always see it in their faces. And then, getting to meet the fans and having them tell me what my music had done for them, that was really something.

I also really enjoyed interacting with both my fans and my dad's fans. I would try to do it to the best of my ability, almost to a fault. I'd do whatever I could—talk to them, take pictures, whatever they wanted. I would spend a lot of time doing that when I was on the road.

I always thought it was important to be gracious and grateful.

My songs can be sad and dark, lonely, depressing. But after the shows, people tell me the songs saved their lives because they could connect—they, too, have been in that place and lived that life. I've had so many people come backstage and tell me that even if what I do is dark, it has literally stopped them from killing themselves. *Oh my God, somebody else feels this way?* I love it when they tell me that. It makes me want to keep doing it.

I saw the pressure of the business from her very first single, "Lights Out." Every time the record company sent it to her for approval it was more countrified, targeting Elvis fans. I remember sitting in her Mercedes, saying, "I liked the original version, but I really don't like this. . . ." The company was resistant to what she wanted, she was resistant to what they wanted, and that's how it went.

I don't like to perform Elvis songs, but I would typically try to do something special for the fans on the anniversary of his death, especially if it was a big year. I did a duet with him called "Don't Cry Daddy" in 1997 as a surprise for the fans, and then a couple of times after that. These performances weren't part of any record, not anything I sold (except for charity once). I feel like my performing his songs was a little cheesy on the one hand, and on the other, I like having my own identity, as much as I can have one.

The one time I performed at Graceland, in 2013, we played three tracks off my *Storm & Grace* album in the Jungle Room. I remember being comfortable, because it was my home, but I also got really anal about all the people in there, the wear and tear of the situation. Oh my God, the carpets . . .

During the making of her second record, *Now What,* she would come home and tell us what every song was about. She recorded the Ramones song "Here Today, Gone Tomorrow" for Johnny Ramone, her good friend who had died a year earlier. "When You Go" was half about me and half about my dad.

But one song, "High Enough," really stands out now. She wasn't doing drugs at the time, but she was drinking—some nights way too much—and the song is very clearly about addiction. But this was way before any of us could have conceived that would become such a problem for her, though in retrospect, storm clouds were gathering even then.

In October 2000, my mother met Nicolas Cage at a birthday party for Johnny Ramone, and on August 10, 2002, they got married in Hawaii. I was thirteen. When she met Nic she had been in a serious relationship for two years with a musician named John Oszajca.

She and John were passionately in love, and they had been engaged for a while, but he was six years younger than she was, and the fact that she had children, and an ex-husband still very much in her life, made it tough for them. Eventually they broke up, and she often wondered how her life would have gone had they not.

Crazy stuff continued. There were further attempts to poison the well with my dad, for example—people close to my grandmother told my mom that Danny had been selling my mom out to the press.

To prove it, they put a PI on my dad for months. At one

point he was playing blackjack for money in Vegas and the PI followed him there. Then, my dad got a call from two of his friends, Cyndi Lauper and Angela McCluskey, to go meet them at Sundance, and even though he was prone to wearing a top hat and was limping around with a cane after he'd hurt his leg on a motorcycle, the PI still managed to lose him and told my mom that they had no idea where he was.

"He's stolen a car and done a runner," the PI said.

At Sundance, my dad met up with Cyndi and Angela and they all went to a party for the French band Air. And who did Danny find at the party? My mother, her boyfriend, and her head of security.

"Hi!" Danny said when he saw my mom.

My mom's jaw dropped. Her PI had lost my dad, but he had found my mom, like he always did.

My mother's relationship with Nic Cage was very short-lived. It felt like something that came in and then left, like a Florida storm—and was, I think, something of a distraction from her breakup with John. She even ping-ponged between Nic and John for a minute. I remember going in her room and Nic was there one day, and then the next day it was John. She clearly couldn't make up her mind.

But Nic and my mom had a ton of fun together. I don't know if they were truly in love, though she said they were. He'd bring her diamonds, and every time he'd come to see her, he'd be in a different car—usually a Lamborghini and always in a different color (I remember a green one, an orange one, a red one, but never the same car twice). My brother, who was seven years old when they met, could never quite pronounce it correctly. He'd say, "Here's Nic in a Lambagini."

Nic bought my mom two really beautiful old cars: a 1959 blue Corvette convertible and a white Cadillac from the sixties. My mom would drive me and Ben to school in them in the morning. I preferred the Corvette because I loved riding with the top down.

On the weekends we'd all get on a yacht and sail to Catalina Island off the southwestern edge of Los Angeles. On one of those trips, she and Nic got into a fight, and her $65,000 engagement ring somehow ended up in the ocean. (She claimed during a later Diane Sawyer interview that it was worth more than that, and also that *she* didn't throw it, but that it was indeed thrown. . . .) A diver was immediately called out to try to find it, but there was no chance—at its deepest, the ocean between Catalina and Los Angeles is three thousand feet.

So Nic bought her another ring, this one even more expensive than the first.

It was on that yacht that I first saw the movie *Jaws*. My mom made me and my brother watch it—she loved horror movies, especially if she could watch them in a scary setting. So, we saw *Jaws* on a yacht in the middle of the ocean, *Misery* while holed up in a ski lodge in Jackson Hole, *The Ring* in Japan, and *Black Christmas* on Christmas night stuck in a cabin at Lake Arrowhead. She and my brother loved it, screaming and laughing all the way through, though it was never my thing. In fact, I was completely traumatized.

It didn't end with movies. One day at school my mom showed up dressed as Michael Myers from *Halloween*. Another time, she came as a dead and bloody Marie Antoinette. We got back at her, though—Ben and I would take turns putting the Michael Myers mask on and chasing each other, and her, around the house. She would be more scared than anyone.

After 108 days, her hurricane of a marriage to Nic Cage was over. In that interview with Diane Sawyer, my mom said of the relationship, "We were so dramatic, the two of us, that we couldn't stay contained."

For most of my life my mother kept a house on the Big Island in Hawaii and spent as much time there as she could. She said she felt a connection to the island and could think more clearly there.

As I've said, my mom always wanted birthdays and holidays to be a big deal, so for my sixteenth birthday celebration a large group of us went to Hawaii: me and six of my closest friends, Ben and two of his friends, my mom and some of her friends, her future husband Michael Lockwood, and my dad.

My mom threw a big party for me on the beach with a guy singing and playing guitar while we ate. My father got me sixteen presents. At some point the guy invited me and my dad to join him on the grass dance floor for a father-daughter dance. My dad and I looked at each other in terror (he was at least four mai tais in, thank God, because fully sober it would have been even more of a nightmare). We were desperate to get out of it, but my mom was adamant because she thought it would be hilarious.

The song the guy chose to accompany the dance was Bob Carlisle's "Butterfly Kisses," the one about the daughter being sent from heaven to be daddy's little girl, one part woman and looking more like her mama every day. Nothing against the song but placing my family members in any type of traditional setting was always going to go poorly. We found the whole thing outrageously hysterical, and my dad and I just gripped on to each other convulsing with laughter. Everyone at the table cracked up. Like Ben, my dad has an incredible laugh, one that's impossible not to laugh along with—honestly, during that dance was the hardest I've ever laughed in my life, and not just because me and my friends had been sneaking our own mai tais and champagne all night.

At the end of the party, we headed back to the house on golf carts to listen to music and keep partying. My mother always had her own bottle of Dom Pérignon that no one was allowed to touch. She loved to dance to seventies music, things like Sister Sledge's "We Are Family" and Van McCoy's "The Hustle," during which she'd force everyone to do the actual hustle. She usually only wanted to play disco . . . oh, and Britney Spears's "Toxic."

She took hip-hop dance classes at our house in Hidden Hills. (She made me do it, too, but I wasn't very good.) She had me do everything with her—at some point she had learned a dance to "Creep" by TLC, and when she dropped me off at a sleepover in the Valley, she stayed to teach me and my friends the moves. She would often hang out with us. She would say, "Your friends are my friends."

At some point that night in Hawaii, "Maggie May" came on and we all shouted along to it, people dancing on tables until the wee hours.

Around three A.M. I took a break, lying on a lawn chair to look at the stars. In Hawaii, anytime you stargaze you'll see shooting stars, and there they were, rushing past my peripheral vision. My mom came to join me, and we lay there together, watching the streaking lights.

I said, "My stomach hurts."

She said, "That's because you've been drinking *my* Dom Pérignon."

Eventually we realized that someone was missing. In the five-minute trip from the beach to the house, we'd somehow managed to lose my dad. This was not uncommon when we were partying as he was always the wild card. But I was slightly worried, so Ben and his friend headed back out to find him—they returned without my dad but with a giant toad they'd discovered.

My mom never worried about my dad. "He'll outlive us all," she would say.

At one point during the dance party, I noticed a figure in the distance approaching our backyard, coming out of the huge, jagged lava rock that loomed behind our house.

My dad was shirtless and had a tiny dot of blood on his nose. No one had any idea how he even managed to make it through the lava or what he had been doing out there. This was not uncommon with Danny. He would just show up with a cheeky smile on his face as though nothing had happened. But *everything* had happened.

The night continued like so many others: My mom and dad dancing together, laughing in their own world. They always felt like a pair of pirates to me.

As I headed off to bed—I could never last as long as my parents—I noticed that my dad had taken off the rest of his clothes and was now sitting naked in a lawn chair, calmly drinking champagne with my mom's security guards.

My mother desperately wanted a normal life, and Michael Lockwood felt like her last shot at it. It seemed that in Michael she felt she'd found a person who could help her stop running from stability.

As my mother began to consider getting married again, she reassessed her relationship with her own mom, and they grew closer, not just for the sake of me and my brother, but for each other. To try to heal what had been done. My mom wrote the song "Raven" for Priscilla:

I'll hear your stories
That filled your sad eyes when you had raven hair
Hold your head up high
I know that I've been ruthless
I've been ruthless
Go on, dry your eyes . . .
Hey, you finally see me
Hi
And I see you
And everything till now
It wasn't that bad really
Beautiful lady
Go on, dry your eyes
You know that I've forgiven you and I'm sorry
And everything till now
It wasn't that bad really
Beautiful lady

My mom wanted to forgive her. And she wanted to own her part in their difficult relationship. Those lyrics meant the world to her mom. After that, Nona would come on tour and get so excited to hear her song. In fact, my grandma and my mom were thick as thieves for a minute. They were always giggling and laughing and having fun and getting drunk together, constantly up to no good.

. . .

In 2005 my mother and Michael got engaged in Hawaii. I remember her coming back to our house in Hidden Hills and showing me the ring in our kitchen.

My mother was in love with Japan and its culture, and she really wanted to have a traditional Japanese wedding, so they married in Kyoto in January 2006.

Around twenty of us traveled to Japan for the ceremony. I was two days late because I had the stomach flu. My dad—who would be the best man at the wedding—waited back and then flew with me to Tokyo.

From Tokyo we all took the train to Kyoto where we stayed in a traditional ryokan. The day after I got into Kyoto, my mom and I had a customary Japanese breakfast of fish, miso soup, and rice, but I ordered a side of white bread and jam because I'd never seen such a fluffy piece of bread in my life. Breakfast over, my best friend and I accompanied my mom and her mom to a dress shop where we all got fitted for traditional wedding kimonos.

At the rehearsal dinner I remember my mom motioning for me to go outside with her. We set off along a beautiful old tiny road (like pretty much every road in Kyoto) together, smoking cigarettes.

During the walk my mom said, "I'm having a panic attack in there—I don't know why. . . ." We walked a little farther and she said, "I felt stuck at that table. I needed to go outside." I was just sixteen at the time, and not sure what was going on, though I figured maybe she was afraid of commitment. Maybe she knew somewhere in her that this was the beginning of the last chapter.

Nevertheless, the next day my mother got married in the backyard of the ryokan. I will always remember how beautiful she looked. After the wedding, we took a train to Hakone and the hot springs of Gora Kadan, on the grounds of Kan'in-no-miya Villa, the former summer villa of a member of the imperial family.

This was one of my mother's favorite places on earth. She loved the hotel and the hot springs. I vividly remember the two of us washing our bodies, sitting on little stools before we entered the baths. We didn't say anything. I think we were both just taking in the beauty that was all around us, and how lucky we felt to be there and with each other.

Later that night we, in our kimonos, went down to the karaoke bar inside the hotel, the one place on the property where it's okay to let go a little bit—in fact, I think it's welcome. Michael Lockwood sang "Let's Dance" by David Bowie, my dad sang "Wild Thing" by the Troggs, my mother and I sang Elton John's "Your

Song" together, then I sang two ABBA songs with my best friend, my mom joining in with "Chiquitita" until the three of us ended up sitting on the floor crying because we were laughing so much.

By the end of the night my dad was dancing with Priscilla, my brother was excitedly running around with his friend, and me and my mom were duetting with the locals, as you do.

My mom desperately wanted more children. She did many rounds of IVF, and eventually she got pregnant.

During her pregnancy with my sisters, she rented a house in Montecito as the first chapter of a sort of fairytale life she wanted to create for herself with her new babies. She was away from L.A., it was a beautiful summer, and we would spend these gorgeous days enjoying her being pregnant in her peaceful garden.

My mom could strongly sense, in a deeply spiritual way, who these two beings inside her were. She felt that Harper would be delicate and feminine and strong, Finley sassy and stubborn and sweet. And she was right. That's who they are.

My mother was like a hurricane. Yet everyone notices how sweet and gentle her kids are.

In October 2008 she gave birth to twin daughters,

my dear sisters, Harper Vivienne Ann Lockwood, named after Michael's mother and Priscilla, and Finley Aaron Love Lockwood, named after Gladys and Elvis.

Harper and Finley were just the sweetest little babies. They were born via C-section at Los Robles Hospital, in Thousand Oaks.

I, along with Michael Lockwood, was present when my mom had her C-section. When they came out, I remember thinking that they looked just how we thought they would. Both of them had the Cupid bow lips and heavy eyelids we all have.

I was nineteen, and they felt like my babies, too.

After my mom's C-section, it was important to get her up and moving as soon as possible, so we'd walk the halls of the hospital together, her hanging on to her little walker. She hated doing it, but to cheer her up, I'd talk to her in this weird language she, Ben, and I had come up with when we were really little. (She'd had something similar with her dad.) If we really wanted to, we could use that language and no one else could understand us. Each day I would come in her room, she'd be grumpy and in pain, and I'd say, "Do you want to stroll the Isles of Robles?" And off we'd go, laughing hysterically.

Eventually the twins came home, and we all set about feeding and burping these two angels. Their father would feed one, my mom would feed the other, and I'd be on burping duty—I usually slept on a cot in the room.

I loved getting up in the night with the babies. We were all so close. If we were at a hotel, my sisters would sleep in bed with my mom, and I would sleep on a cot at their feet. We were always in the same room together.

My mom was so intuitive and instinctual when it came to being a mother. She knew instantly that Finley liked to be held this way, and Harper that way. I don't know where she got it from—I don't think it was something that had been passed on to her necessarily, I think she was born that way. Circumstances shape a person, but there's a part of you that's your spirit, and my mom's spirit was brimming with maternal love.

For years, she had wanted another chance to be a mother. With me and Ben, she had been a young mom—this time she wanted to do it over and be more thoughtful about it and spend more time with her kids. She didn't want tons of staff and nannies raising them. She wanted to do it all herself, hands on.

Ben's and my childhoods were perfect, amazing, and yet my mom still wanted to do a better job the second time around, to be even more present and do everything herself. So she concocted a plan: She was going to sell the L.A. house and move to England and have a beautiful life in the country where my sisters would have a country garden where they could go for walks every morning and would grow up with cute British accents.

This is one of the most heartbreaking things about the last decade of her life—being a mother was the most important thing to her, she had really wanted another chance at it, and yet her addiction showed up.

Her father had been an addict, but there was scant awareness of it in the 1970s. Back then, everyone in Hollywood seemed to be an addict, but no one had language for it. Elvis had thought he was just doing what his doctors advised—if the doctor told him to take a drug to go to sleep and one to wake up, that's what he did. His intentions were pure. So there might have been a genetic component to my mom's addiction—either way, it just waited around all her life until right after my sisters were born.

And then it showed up and burned everything down.

My mother's life soon got to a point where she began to feel out of control. She had so many staff, running everything for her, that she didn't know simple things like how to turn on the living room TV. She had had a great run, a whole decade of letting people in, trusting them. Yet money was a part of her life that she had virtually no awareness about. One day she caught wind that a certain staff member had maybe misused the company credit card. She began to look into it and found that some staff members were overcharging her cards in ways she didn't feel good about—too many flights purchased, too many new phones, too many pizzas. Most of these staff members were also her best friends. They weren't thieves, maybe they just got a little lazy. But for my mother it released the dormant feeling that everyone around her had an agenda. Even deeper than that, she thought she was unlovable. The way she would handle these feelings was to exile people, regardless of how big or small the offense.

At the end of that idyllic ten years, virtually overnight, my mother had let everybody go at Hidden Hills—friends, security, assistants, people she had known and loved for years. Her religion. She just suddenly wanted everything gone.

One by one, they were sent away. The only people who remained were her children, Michael Lockwood, and, of course, my dad.

Something in her heart had never left Graceland, hadn't emotionally developed past when her father died. She said herself how much she wanted friends, but after nearly forty years of continuous letdowns—people selling her out to the press, being irresponsible with her money, dating her for the wrong reasons—she learned to cut people out of her life and not look back.

For the first time in her life, she wanted to be alone.

One day, she left the house by herself, which she never did, and went to a little independent theater in Woodland Hills to watch any movie she could find—they happened to be showing *Into the Wild*. She didn't know anything about the film ahead of time. Her seeing that movie is the first thing I remember my mother ever doing by herself. I was concerned, but I also remember thinking, *What a serendipitous movie to have come upon, a film about a young, idealistic man, setting out into the wilderness on his own, finding his identity through isolation.*

But it ends in tragedy.

I can get really mean and really angry and I freak people out when I get like that. It comes from trying to protect myself from pain. I just push people the fuck away. It's the fear of being hurt. I know people can hurt me, so I'll shut them out.

I learned from the best: Michael Jackson. He did it really well.

But even as a child, I remember being really angry with my aunt one time and I said, "I disown you—don't ever talk to me again." My aunt! I'm super sensitive and scared and not secure with who I am. I don't know who I am—I never really got the chance to uncover my own identity. I didn't have a family. I didn't have a childhood, and though some of it was fun, there was also constant trouble.

And then I woke up. I woke up about a lot of stuff that had been going on around me for years. A lot of people were invested in having me quiet and manageable.

By then, unbeknownst to all of us, she was regularly taking the opioids prescribed to her after the C-section she'd had for my sisters' birth.

SEVEN

THE BUS FROM NASHVILLE TO L.A.

If you don't have something to keep you focused, or some kind of purpose, it's hard out there. Life is not easy. Who doesn't want to be high? Drugs or drinking make you feel great.

You have to have something bigger, bigger than that feeling of being high, bigger than that happiness, bigger than that emptiness. If you don't, you're in trouble.

Before I became addicted, I was focused. I wanted to know what the fuck I was doing here, I wanted to know about life, I wanted to know about people. For a long time, I didn't want to fuck around. I needed answers, whatever they were. That had been my focus.

But as soon as that was gone, I was off the rails. When I had my twins and I was in the hospital and they gave me Norco, that's when I felt the first oh-my-God high from a painkiller.

I was forty.

I don't really know what I was doing, to be honest. I was getting isolated, slowly starting to get rid of everyone and everything in my life, all the pillars I had set up,

all the people and the friends and the relationships. I was starting to, one by one, dislodge and dismantle each and every one of those things.

My mother had started by taking opioids for pain after her C-section, and then she progressed to taking them to sleep.

She had turned forty in February 2008; my sisters were born in October that same year (I would turn twenty the following May). After her brief stint with drugs as a teenager she had never touched them again. She drank, but, like she said, as an adult she wouldn't even take Advil or Tylenol.

Throughout my life she would often say, "If I tried drugs, it would be over for me." I see now that that was such a strong hint to an addiction issue she had an intuition about. I think it was subconscious, but it stalked her. She had been holding it back with Scientology, with raising children, with marriages, with spirituality. But it was there, like a shadow, the whole time. She'd say, "My dad was forty-two when he died. I'm thirty-nine. . . ."

We never could have imagined it would be something that would come for her so viciously, so late in life.

. . .

Shortly after my sisters were born, to try to gain some agency, my mom moved with them and Michael Lockwood to England.

Initially, they lived briefly in southwest London, Richmond, and some days she would take my sisters in their stroller to a little crepe restaurant on the Thames. My mom loved the quaint life she was creating for herself.

Ben and I felt a bit abandoned because her move to England meant that for the first time we didn't all live together in the same house. She got us a house in Calabasas, but we pretty much stayed in England with her most of the time.

My mom had originally thought about living in Ireland—we would go to Ireland a lot when we were younger. My mom was friends with the Austrian-Irish artist Gottfried Helnwein, and we'd stay at his castle, Castle Gurteen de La Poer, in Kilsheelan, a few miles east of Clonmel. We'd all go to the local pubs and dance to the music, and then when closing time came, we'd head back to Gurteen and run around the castle grounds, or climb a spiral tower to the top and lay under the stars, me drunk at seventeen, until the sun peered through the crenellations.

So my mom had really wanted to move to Ireland, but

every property she found she claimed was haunted. She had a very practical and pragmatic connection to ghosts, past lives, spirits. One day a realtor took us to a very old house somewhere outside of Cork. She led us down a hallway with pink floral wallpaper and a very low ceiling. Before we even reached the living room, my mom said, "It's haunted," turned around, and walked right out.

She soon settled on England instead. In the beginning, England, like Hidden Hills before it, was really magical—the first couple of years especially. It seemed to me that she thought this was her last shot at stability, once more having children and living in a huge country house in the middle of nowhere. Again she was trying to re-create what she had felt with my father. A simple life without all of the people. Just her husband and her children.

After Richmond, in 2010, she bought a fifteenth-century property in Rotherfield, about thirty miles northeast of Brighton on the south coast. The house had fifty acres, a gorgeous lake, sheep, horses, topiary, even an orangery—it was truly beautiful, stunning.

It was also haunted, but only in one room. Finley told my mother and Michael that she often saw a man in her bedroom. Eventually my mother and Michael got more details: Apparently, the great-grandmother of a resident of the house had lived—and died—in the house. And the loud bangs that they all regularly heard around midnight were probably to do with the great-grandfather who had shot himself in the barn many years earlier—the same barn that was now their living room.

My mom got very into gardening in England. She would plant radishes, potatoes, and carrots in the garden with my sisters. It was also the first time she cooked—she still had a chef, but she had more time on her hands so spent some of it in the kitchen. We would take tea by the fire all day, too—she loved making and stoking fires. She would just sit there and intently watch the flames, trying to predict them. No one could make a fire blaze like my mother—she was a fire witch.

Every weekend Ben and I would take the train up to London to meet up with our friends. At Christmastime we'd head to Harrods in Knightsbridge or to the Borough Market in Southwark, do our Christmas shopping, then head back to our local pub in Crowborough, a few miles from the house, to hang out with the locals and sing and dance till the wee hours of the morning. (By this time my mom had become close friends with the owners of the pub so we could skirt the eleven P.M. closing bell and stay all night.) Ben was eighteen and sometimes he'd work behind the bar.

This was my mom's idea of living a small life—she still had a house manager, one security guard, one driver, a chef, and two nannies for the girls, which sounds like a lot, but was a skeleton crew compared to what had been going on in California. Eventually she'd create her own pub at the house, where a bunch of the locals, including some new friends like guitarist Jeff Beck, his wife Sandra, and Sarah Ferguson, could hang out. (Sarah and my mom had a real loyalty toward each other—they'd both been through similar onslaughts in the press and in life, torn apart and shamed simply for being women who were unapologetically themselves.) And my mom had huge Christmas parties, too. Mostly, though, she liked going to the chip shop and having a roast on Sundays and gardening with my sisters.

Seemingly she had done what she set out to do: She had created a very sweet little life in the countryside. So the first couple years were truly magical.

We had no idea, though, that her pill use was very slowly increasing.

One night we all went up to London to hang out at Soho House. Typically, when my mother and I got into fights they would resolve themselves fairly quickly. She could be rational, could take responsibility, and be empathetic. That night at Soho House, though, was the first time I realized something was wrong.

It began as a small argument about me wanting to go to Ireland before Christmas, but quickly I felt a viciousness from her I had never felt before. She wouldn't resolve the argument, and the back-and-forth felt very irrational.

"You didn't tell me you were going to Ireland this close to Christmas," she said.

"Yes, I *did* tell you," I said, "you just don't remember."

She ignored that.

"So, you're going to leave me here and take your brother to Ireland? That's just so not right, so not okay to do that."

"I just *told* you: I told you *weeks* ago we were going to Ireland. I'm so confused right now. . . ."

She became relentless; she wouldn't let it go. There was a new meanness in her where before we would have resolved it quickly.

I was so confused and angry at the exchange that I stormed out of the club. It had made me feel crazy. On my way out I found my brother having a cigarette.

"Mom is being so weird. . . ." I said.

"What do you mean?" he said.

"Like, she's just getting mad that we're going to Ireland when we already told her weeks ago. She won't let it go."

I was dressed in a fancy gown, and I had nowhere to go—it was two A.M. As I walked away, a rickshaw passed me, and I got in. The rickshaw was all decked out in Christmas lights, and the guy was blasting "Angels" by Robbie Williams so loud I couldn't hear myself think. There I was, dressed in a floor-length gown and faux fur coat, and even in my fury I couldn't help but see the absurdity of the situation and laugh at myself. I texted my mom a video of me riding through Oxford Circus as the song blasted. My mother sent a text back: "Hah!" After fights, we wouldn't typically have a conversation to resolve the fight. Eventually one person would just break the silence and it was back to business as usual—this was that text. I headed back to Soho House.

But things were changing. And not just with my mom.

After a couple of years of living in England, we all went to Hawaii on vacation, and that's when my mom admitted to me that yes, she was addicted to opioids, but that she was planning on going to rehab in Mexico. Me and my brother and sisters went to Mexico with her.

Halfway through, though, she made an excuse to cut it short.

"I'm going to have to go back—the girls are starting school after Easter," she said.

"What do you mean?" I said. "Surely you knew this was landing on those dates?"

"Yeah, but they just started. They have all these new friends. They have their routine. I'm not going to pull them out of that. . . ."

"I think everyone would agree that you staying here is more important than my sisters missing a week of school," I said, but she was adamant. She always did what she wanted to do. My brother and I were angry, but we couldn't change her mind.

Back in England, there was a tacit awareness between me, my brother, and Michael that maybe my mother didn't *want* to get sober. She was always extremely honest, but I think she felt that being honest was the virtue rather than the changing of her behavior. Since she had admitted it to us, the honesty seemed to give her the license to continue with her addiction.

Now that we knew, my brother and I noticed things, like she would fall asleep too early when we watched movies together.

One morning I was sitting in the kitchen drinking tea, and as my mom came by, she slightly bumped into the wall as she passed. I felt a sense of dread because I knew from her telling me for years and years that if she ever did heroin, it would kill her. She would say, "I would never just dabble; if I did it, it would take me out."

Eventually she realized that moving to England hadn't been such a good idea. She had distanced herself from all of her friends, and the drug use had increased along with the loneliness and isolation. Or she needed to be alone to take the drugs. Or both.

Her community was gone. She was in the English countryside with two babies and no friends. She decided that isolation was the problem. She hated L.A. and wanted to be closer to Graceland, so she decided she was going to move to Nashville to be more social, and make a new record.

I felt better. This felt like she had a plan. Danny was going to try to sell the house in England, and she was going to get off the pills and start over in Nashville.

While she looked for Nashville homes, she rented a house in L.A. on a golf course with a beautiful backyard, a pool, and a movie room where my brother and I would watch *Game of Thrones*.

One night I went downstairs to get a drink and I noticed that Michael was taking my sisters out of the house to Chuck E. Cheese. It was strange that my mom wasn't going with them. I went upstairs to find her and headed into her room. I realized that she was hiding in her bathroom.

"Don't come in," she said.

I ignored her.

When I entered, I found her crying in her bathtub. She had a black eye and a bloody nose—she'd fallen while high. She was sobbing and clearly felt ashamed. She'd told Michael to take my sisters out so that they wouldn't see her face.

She knew this had all gone too far. She went back to rehab the following week.

After that stint, she then flew to Nashville.

My mother was slowly falling apart. My brother was, too.

We were all drinking a lot, but even when he drank, my brother remained jovial, fun. He was somebody who never wanted the night to end, the last person awake.

But there was one night at a club when I was around twenty-two and Ben started pushing me to leave. It didn't feel right. He got me in a taxi and sent me back to the hotel where we were staying for the weekend. Only later did I realize he'd been doing drugs—probably

Molly or coke—and he had wanted me out of there so he could do whatever he wanted without me finding out.

This became a theme in my family: They would do things behind my back. I was kind of the narc—my mom always said I was too harsh on Ben or too harsh on her, but I think it was simply that I was the only one who wasn't an addict—so I was the downer.

But I was getting concerned about Ben. One night around that time, he was drinking at the pub, came back late, and fell off his bed and chipped his front tooth. He cried in my mom's arms that night at the bottom of the stairs.

Still, he never really drank during the day. He was a binge drinker, going hard for a couple of weeks and then stopping for a long stretch. We got a lot of time with him sober. I would worry about him in the moment, but then the following week or month he'd be fine, better than fine—drinking green juices and working out.

It didn't affect my relationship with him, but my mom's addiction meant she was simply not there emotionally a lot of the time.

When I started talking to a therapist, it was really nice to hear somebody talk back and say, "Hey, you're not fucked up," or "You need to stop shooting yourself in the foot."

I also attended group therapy and initially I really resisted it. But eventually I started getting close to people. I realized that they were all as fucked up as me.

I didn't love AA. You talk about drugs and alcohol all the time and it drives me fucking crazy. I agree that I am powerless over it and I believe that I could stop everything, but the pills were designed to addict you from within. Even if you only take them for two or three weeks straight, you're going to have some kind of blowback. Your body's going to withdraw.

But I don't think it's just physical. I believe that a body is just a body, and the spirit is ultimately inside of the physical shell, and I don't think chemicals have anything to do with the spirit. They make the physical addiction to the body—but the root of the addiction comes from being really unhappy. That's a spiritual problem.

After I left Scientology, I started upping the pills. I thought, *Oh my God, I've lost my religion and it's been my only pavement to walk on, my replacement family*. Everything was gone—all my friends, everything.

I knew it was over.

And I was so devastated, I used the drugs as a coping mechanism.

Two weeks into her new life in Nashville my mother was back on opioids.

The addiction got worse. She was drinking more, taking more opioids. At one point she found an article that said cocaine can help people get off opioids, so she began to do cocaine to get off the opioids and then opioids to get off the cocaine. Her addiction would continue through all of the stints in rehab on the basis that she was always in severe and life-threatening withdrawals that no doctor could understand. She felt all of the doctors were too harsh. They wouldn't give her enough of what she needed, so she was "doing it herself."

It escalated to eighty pills a day.

It took more and more to get high, and I honestly don't know when your body decides it can't deal with it anymore. But it does decide that at some point.

I believe that we're all born innocent, and that everyone's nature is innately good, but they get fucked by their surroundings. And I believe that my brain is different, that I am an addict. Otherwise I wouldn't have had all those years in between being a stupid teenager to suddenly getting a drug habit at forty.

For a couple of years it was recreational and then it wasn't. It was an absolute matter of addiction, withdrawal in the big leagues. If I had fully run out of drugs, the severity of the withdrawal would have left me either in the hospital or dead. My blood pressure would shoot up so high.

I just wanted to check out. It was too painful to be sober.

My whole life had blown up, it felt like one thing after another, and I could not take any more beatings.

My mom came up with all kinds of reasons why she didn't want to get off drugs, but I think one of the most poignant ones was her feeling of shame about becoming an addict with two young children. Her parenting standards were so high that I don't think she could ever truly get sober knowing what she had put my sisters through. The one thing that she had always really prided herself on was that she was a great mother. She said, "My music wasn't that successful, I didn't finish high school, I'm not beautiful, I'm not good enough—but I'm a great mother."

When she started to feel like she wasn't even that, she couldn't handle it, so she doubled down.

When she lived in Nashville, in the depths of her addiction, my mom would often drive the two hundred miles southwest to Graceland to sleep in her dad's bed. It seemed like the only place she found any comfort.

Often, she would take me, Ben, and my sisters upstairs to his room and we would all sleep in her dad's bed while there were tours going on downstairs. I wish this was a magical time in a magical family place. But the truth of it was, she was in the house desperate to feel protected, desperate to connect with her father. She would lie in his bed, lie on his floor, anything to feel some comfort. It was the feeling of going to church when all is lost and saying, "Please, Jesus, help me."

And every time she went, she'd point out an empty plot of grass where she would eventually be laid to rest, next to her father in the Meditation Garden.

. . .

When I was back in L.A., I got a call from my mother.

"There's something wrong with me. Physically," she said.

"You need to come to L.A.," I said. "We need to get you to a hospital."

That began a long text chain between me and my brother in L.A. and my mom in Nashville, excerpts of which I offer here:

Mom: Please come get me out of here ASAP. We can find a trailer or something. We can get to California. I'm not kidding. I need you both. I don't have the strength to leave. I'm not well in any way. My legs and body are swollen. I spit up blood. My ankles are twisted. My lips are bleeding. I throw up everything but yogurt. My feet are so swollen I'm scared.

Me: You need to go to the doctor now! You need to get checked up and vitamins. Go to the doctor now. This is not okay.

Ben: She doesn't want to go to a doc. There's a doc that will go to the house. That's the best move right now.

Me: [My mom's assistant] Christy and Lockwood are both saying you won't go to the doctor. You need to go to the doctor.

Mom: Not a doctor here. Tennessee has strong laws. They'll take away my babies.

Me: For drugs? Who cares? You're going to die. Mom, you just need a doctor to check your vitals.

Ben: I don't care if the devil himself came to earth and said he was a doctor, as long as he's a doctor.

Mom: I have my doctors in L.A. I want to see.

Me: Can I please get you an RV to drive you to L.A. tomorrow?

Ben: Get in an RV and come here.

Me: Mom, I'm booking an RV in Tennessee tomorrow. Ben will [fly to Nashville and] go with you and the babies.

Ben: Answer, Mom.

Ben: Mom, answer my fucking phone call. I've called you 21 times. If you don't want to talk to me that's fine but I have a plan.

Me: Mom, Ben has a good plan. You'll take an RV with the babies.

Mom: Where do we stay?

Me: I'll find you somewhere.

Ben: Call me.

Call me.

Call me.

Call me.

Call me.

Call me.

Call me.

Call me.

Call me.

Call me.

Call me.

I had done a bunch of blow and a shot of tequila and a bunch of pills. All that was mixed with stress.

I was really unhappy and my body was not doing well.

Riley and Ben wanted to get me to a doctor—everyone wanted to get me to the doctor, but I wouldn't go to one in Nashville—so Riley sent Ben to get me because my assistant, Christy, had told her that a couple of times she thought I had gone, that I had looked dead on the bed.

Ben showed up and he, the girls, and I took a tour bus all the way from Nashville to L.A. We drove because I wanted to do cocaine the whole time and couldn't if I was on an airplane. I didn't think I could even get through airport security. The tour bus had six beds, a bedroom in the back, a kitchen.

When we arrived in L.A., I went straight in to see the head of Cedars-Sinai. I was at thirty heartbeats per minute. I lay there scared to death.

My echocardiogram came back bad. I was literally losing my heart. My heart was dead, just in pieces.

When she arrived in L.A. from Nashville, Mom's head and face were twice their normal size. She went straight from the emergency room to the ICU—she was in heart failure. It was chaos, and in the midst of it, she told Michael Lockwood she was leaving him.

It took about a week for her to start to recover.

Once she was feeling a bit better, she was desperate to find somewhere safe, somewhere gated, to live. She repeatedly asked if we could find somewhere on Mountaingate, where we'd all lived when I was little, where we'd lost Jaco the pug but where we'd been so happy. . . .

My mother had changed business management at that time and somehow all of her credit cards had been frozen. She had nothing. Everything was a mess. She went to court-ordered rehab in L.A., submitted to court-ordered pee tests, the whole bit. The rehab gave her Suboxone and other drugs like Seroquel and gabapentin to wean her off the opioids, but they only served to make her even more high because whatever the normal dose was, she would somehow get five times that amount from the doctors.

When I would go visit her, she didn't even know who I was. I remember sitting with her while she tried to light her cigarette for five full minutes. Unsuccessfully. It was as if it was all happening in slow motion. The cigarette was never closer than a foot away from the lighter.

While in rehab, my mom had decided to get bariatric surgery. Her entire life she had been harassed for being fat. The surgery was something she'd always wanted.

It was a strange time to decide to have surgery, in rehab. She wasn't done with her program. I remember worrying that it was a way to stay on medication a little bit longer. I didn't feel she was ready to be sober. If you have any experience with addicts, you'll know that when I questioned her about the timing of the surgery, it turned into a massive fight. That was a dead giveaway. Then she removed me from the guest list at the hospital. In the midst of her addiction, I was a narc to her—I was Pookie (her regular name for me, I was seldom if ever Riley), not a pirate.

I often found myself calling out her attempts to best the system. I would contact the doctors behind her back and tell them that they were overprescribing. But she was Lisa Marie Presley, and so she almost always prevailed, and was furious that I'd tried to intervene. Bending doctors, anyone, to her will was a celebrity phenomenon that she was very aware of. She often told me that the issue with her father, and with Michael Jackson, was that everyone around them always just said yes—but of course she didn't see the issue the same way when she was doing it herself. In the throes of her addiction, if you wanted to stop her, you were out. To me she would say, "You don't understand. You're not an addict."

Soon she was out of rehab, but incredibly depressed. She'd been through another separation, and she felt like she had nothing to live for, nothing to look forward to. She was on a bunch of medications that left her numb. All she could really do was sit on the couch and watch TV.

For her to be able to see my sisters, there had to be a court-certified monitor present. I was that monitor, so for my sisters to move back in with her, my mom had to live with me. And as my brother lived with her, I got my brother as a bonus. So my mom, my sisters, and my brother moved into my two-thousand-square-foot house in the Valley.

Then my dad moved in, too.

It seemed like it could have been good to have everyone together.

But it felt like the end of things.

We'd had this amazing, colorful, beautiful, abundant, fun, joyful life, but in that house, it took a turn and got unbearably dark, for all of us.

Japan was my brother's favorite country. When Ben and I were on the train to Kyoto one day he said to me, half-joking, kind of coyly, "It's so hard because when I do something new, I get really good at it so fast that it becomes uninspiring." Nothing kept his interest long because when he learned to do something, he actually *would* be good at it. He was one of those people who could annoyingly be great at everything. But he hadn't found the one thing that really grabbed him. He'd wanted to play guitar for a living, he'd taken business courses, he'd trained to be a sushi chef, even got a chef's knife tattooed on one arm, but nothing ever stuck. He was really smart—way more academic than I was. In his mid-twenties, he began to feel pressure to make a choice. I was always trying to help him figure out what to do with his life. "You could move to Hawaii and fish," I'd say, another passion of his. We'd send each other links to houses on Redfin that he might one day buy. His dream was to live a simple life somewhere—Hawaii or Japan were his top choices.

But when the conversation would progress, he'd always hit his reality: "I can't leave Mom."

He, like the rest of us siblings, was privy to the tremendously deep sadness and loneliness of her. How she had ended up pushing away virtually everyone and everything she loved and was very much alone. And he'd given himself the responsibility of never leaving her side.

In May 2018, I went to Tokyo to film a movie for Netflix called *Earthquake Bird* and Ben came with me.

Initially we stayed in the Park Hyatt, the hotel that features in *Lost in Translation*. I'm not much of a drinker, but on my twenty-ninth birthday, I got way too drunk—I can *not* handle my alcohol—and threw up over the side of the hotel. I could hear my parents' voices in my head telling me what a lightweight I was. I probably only had three drinks.

In a family of pirates, that's not necessarily a bad thing to be. My family took pride in their piracy, and they really lived up to it, but as my mother once said when I claimed I was hardcore, "Oh, Pookie, you are *so* not hardcore."

The next week, we found an apartment to live in.

Ben and I had the most beautiful time in Japan that month. We would wake up every day and head to the sauna or the steam room. Then we'd take a walk to get smoothies and just keep wandering.

I had some yellow Nikes I wore around the city that he was obsessed with. He never wanted anything I had other than those shoes.

I didn't have too much to do in the movie, so there was time. I had an assistant, Shusaku, and he and Ben became best friends. When I did have to work, the two of them would run around the city together. Tokyo is a beautiful place for ceramics, so we went to ceramics classes, the three of us—we made so many pots and bowls and cups, Shu translating for us.

Ben was a foodie. We'd go out to all these incredible omakase restaurants, and he would eat everything and anything. There were dishes that I would *not* eat—sea urchin, for example—but with the chef right there, I didn't want to be rude, so I'd wait for the chef to look away and then slip whatever it was I couldn't stomach to Ben.

Despite Ben being so into the best food, one of his

favorite things to eat were rice balls from 7-Eleven. (In fairness, the food at 7-Elevens in Japan is very good.) We'd take the rice balls to Zushi Beach, a surfer beach about an hour south of the city. We'd climb the mountain to a shrine, me in my bright yellow Nike sneakers—"banana shoes," as Ben called them—and eat the rice balls.

Ben would give me a hard time about the shoes every day. "Did you get my banana shoes yet?" he'd ask repeatedly.

And I promised over and over that I'd get him a pair.

For a while Ben got heavily into making jewelry.

A few weeks after I started dating the man who would become my husband, Ben Smith-Petersen, we were all in Ireland together. Ben Ben told Ben (my mom later christened the two "Ben Ben" and "Big Ben" to differentiate) that it was obvious that he was going to propose to me—we were children, but we were clearly going to be together—and that he'd make a ring. A few weeks later Big Ben was in Australia visiting his mom. She mentioned that she had some diamonds that she'd taken out of her great-grandmother's ring—she'd intended to repurpose them into something for herself, but she gave him one of them. Back in the States, Ben

Ben found a vintage ring with no setting, and set the diamond for Big Ben.

Big Ben then attached the ring to our dog, and told me to call him over. And that's how he—well, technically, the dog—proposed.

Back in L.A., while trying to look after our mother, Ben Ben's own addiction to alcohol was growing.

And as it grew, so did his depression. Though he suffered from anxiety sober or not, when he wasn't drinking, he was often fine. His depression didn't seem dangerous; he would sometimes go on a bender and he would sometimes do drugs, take Molly for a week and feel the comedown, but after a few days away from it, he was back to normal.

My mom was such a powerful person that whatever she was doing really affected all of us. Our lives were dictated by the tone she was setting, and that tone became very heavy and hopeless. Our mom, the queen, the fiercest of family leaders, had fallen down. I had mistakenly thought she was so strong-minded that nothing could ever truly hobble her. But of course it could. Enough pain can hobble anyone. She'd been addicted to drugs for the better part of a decade and the drugs created a sense of hopelessness that permeated everything. She stopped wanting to do anything. She felt like her life was over. She'd say, "I have nothing—I have no husband, I have no friends, I have no life." She was bottoming out.

Ben Ben was a mama's boy through and through, and he couldn't handle his mama being in pain. They were so close—like Elvis and Gladys—one inextricably tied to the rise and fall of the other, and seeing each other in pain was impossibly hard for them. It wrecked him. What had once felt like a perfect childhood to us gave way to what felt like a nightmare to him. Like many in our family, substances were where Ben found relief, and his alcohol addiction got worse.

Sometimes I'd think, *Well, he doesn't seem like he's drinking that much more than other friends of mine.* In fact, from that standpoint, he was not even the one I was most concerned about.

We were still very tight, but he didn't tell me how bad he was really feeling. One day he told my mom that he didn't think that he was mentally okay, but she didn't tell me that. And you wouldn't have known unless he told you.

We were *all* very close, forever cuddling, curled up in bed together. So when it got dark, how could it not affect all of us? All our lives my mother had been leading the way, and none of us could get used to her not having her usual strength.

The drugs she stayed on after rehab were dimming her light.

The following year, my mom was able to move into her own house in Calabasas, and my brother and sisters moved in with her.

I swear that house was haunted. It felt cursed. Or maybe it was how powerful my mother's moods had become.

She wouldn't go a few days without seeing me, but I didn't want to be there. The house felt so heavy. My brother could feel it, anyone who went there could feel it.

Ben Ben finally decided he was drinking too much so my mom sent him to rehab.

But on his return, he was still stuck in that terrible house watching his mother struggle. She was not truly sober, either—she wasn't taking narcotics, but she was certainly getting high on the post-rehab cocktail. We would fight about it all the time, and she would get vicious, protecting her addiction. Otherwise, she would just sleep on the couch all day. It was incredibly hard for my brother to watch.

Then she had a seizure. My brother and her assistant were home with her at the time—Ben Ben stayed by her side until the paramedics arrived.

I showed up that night to take care of my sisters. My mom was in the hospital. Ben was sitting on the couch in silence.

"Are you okay?" I asked.

"Yep," he said, as though he was completely checked out.

I had my attention on the twins—they had just seen the paramedics wheel their mother out and were very upset—so I wasn't able to check on my brother.

After the seizure, my mother realized she couldn't do this anymore. Though she remained on mood stabilizers, she did manage to truly sober up. One day she said to me, "That's enough. I really need to change my life."

She had been very chastened by the seizure—in fact, she had a deep phobia about them. One time, in a mall in Florida when I was around seven years old, a man was having a violent seizure on the floor. My mother couldn't shake the image of it for months, and eventually had to get therapy about it.

When she told me that she'd had enough, I remember

thinking, *Finally*. Her addiction was going to be gone. I really felt it was.

But I noticed that my brother's disposition changed after the seizure. He seemed quieter and was often alone in his room. I remember feeling like I wanted to check on him more than usual, because I knew that seeing his mother have a seizure would have been unbearable for him.

That haunted house in Calabasas had developed a minor mold problem, so my mom, Ben, and my sisters were staying at the Beverly Hills Hotel while the problem was remediated—my mom was badly allergic to mold.

During their stay, Ben went back to the house one night to throw a birthday party for his girlfriend.

My mom and Ben were texting back and forth that night. She had picked up something about his mindset, something that worried her.

"Are you coming back tomorrow? Come home," she wrote.

At the house, the party went into the small hours. Everyone was happily hanging out downstairs.

Ben went upstairs around three-thirty A.M.

"Come home," she wrote.

He said he was just going to get a beer.

EIGHT

BEN BEN

No one in the house heard the gunshot. It took almost an hour for people to realize Ben hadn't returned. Upstairs, they found the door was locked. They had to break in.

When I was thirteen, I had a best friend at school named Brian.

One day, I remember coming to school, and everybody was being weird. They called us into a room and told us that Brian had died from sniffing glue. We were freaking out, so they took us for a walk to get our attention outward.

But they had lied to us. I remember saying to a teacher on that walk, "How did he really do it?"

The teacher said, "He shot himself."

. . .

People have misconceptions about suicide. I always thought if someone is talking about it, they won't do it.

It was five-thirty A.M., July 12, 2020. My phone was ringing.

Half awake, startled, I said to my husband, "Christy's calling me, something's wrong." If my mom's assistant was calling me that early, it had to be serious. *Oh God, something happened to my mom,* I thought.

My husband said, "Pick it up."

My heart started beating so hard I could feel the blood in my ears, and I picked up.

"Your brother shot himself in the head! Your brother shot himself in the head!" Christy kept saying, over and over.

I could not take it in. I could hear her saying it, but I could not absorb the words, the finality of that statement. I was suddenly filled with the most profoundly painful thought: *This is real and there's nothing I can do.*

Time started to stretch, or quicken, I couldn't tell, but my next thought was that I was about to have to tell my mom that the second man she loved the most in the world was gone.

I don't remember getting off the phone. Somehow, we got into the car. I was drinking a yellow Gatorade, and I lit a cigarette. My husband was at the wheel. That drive felt like it lasted seven years. And that's all I remember about that drive: a drink, the cigarette, and an eternity.

My mother was asleep in her hotel room. She slept with a white noise machine, which was the only way she could get any rest. I ran to her suite and started pounding on the door. Nothing. After a few minutes I called the hotel lobby and begged them to let me into her room. The security guy came and I started freaking out.

"I have to get in there right now."

"We can't let you in there," he said.

"Please, please, let me in. Please. You have to. I need to talk to my mom. It's an emergency."

"We can't let you in without her approving it," he said.

I started pounding even harder on the door. The thought flashed in my head: *This will be the end of her life, when I tell her this.* I already knew, clear as day, in those moments banging on her door, that any time I got with her after what was about to happen would be a gift. A bonus. I couldn't imagine her living without my brother.

Finally, I heard my mom's footsteps approaching.

The door opened, she was half asleep.

"What's going on?" she said.

I took a breath.

"Ben Ben shot himself in the head," I said. I tried to say it calmly.

She didn't understand what I had said. Nothing registered on her face. I said it again. Nothing. We just kind of looked at each other. Then she started grabbing her things and said, "I need to go to him now."

She went into the room where my sisters were sleeping.

"I have to go," she said, "something's happened to Ben Ben."

They asked if he was going to be okay.

"No," she said.

They immediately started crying. But we had to leave them with the babysitter, we couldn't stay.

Then I had to tell my father. He was in Oregon. I barely remember the call. I think I said the same thing I'd been told: "Ben Ben shot himself in the head."

He just said, "What?" It didn't make sense to any of us. My father immediately drove to the Portland airport and flew to L.A.

We got in the car and drove from her hotel in Beverly Hills back to her house in Calabasas. I was lying across the backseat, my body in deep panic. I couldn't breathe. The car eternity returned.

Then I could hear myself breathing and it sounded so loud.

We pulled up to my mom's house and the police had already barricaded it off with yellow caution tape. It was a crime scene. We went up to his room. There were police everywhere, in every room and hallway of the house. A police officer stood in front of his door. My mother wanted to go in there and see him, but the officer wouldn't let us, so we went into my mom's room to wait. I had to lie on the floor—I couldn't hold my body up. My mom and I sat on her floor together.

It was too painful to cry. I distinctly remember thinking, *I've never seen this in a movie, when someone dies, how it's too painful to cry*.

And when you do eventually cry, it's a different cry. It feels like something deeper than your emotions is crying out, and it feels like it's never going to end. Some kind of a terrifying, bottomless pain.

We had to wait about two or three hours while the police investigated to make sure there was no foul play. We barely spoke.

Finally, one of the officers said, "We don't typically do this, but we'll let you see him." My mother waited at the bottom of the stairs desperately. About thirty minutes later, they rolled him in front of us and unzipped the body bag.

His face was perfectly intact, beautiful somehow. He had bruises under his eyes and what looked like wine stains on his mouth. He had this little smile on his face. My mom grabbed his head. "What did you do, Benjamin? What did you do?" she said, as though he could hear her.

That was the first time she cried.

She had blood all over her hands from holding the back of his head. Then she had blood all over her face.

She kissed his forehead and held her face to his and cried.

I was in shock. I left my body entirely.

I think I was crying but I don't know. I felt like I was being piloted by some other force. I was afraid to touch him. I put my hand on the body bag around his chest. I wish that I'd hugged him right there, one more time.

They zipped up the body bag and took him outside. We followed. They loaded him into the back of a car and slammed the doors. And then he was just in there and then they just drove him away. Just like that.

I don't really know how else to describe watching my little brother, my parents' only son, being driven away in a coroner's van, forever.

The van just drives away, and you just watch it go.

. . .

My father moved into my mother's new rental house with us the next day.

For two weeks I couldn't really remember how to talk. I could understand what words were, but I couldn't understand how to get them from my thoughts to my lips. People would talk to me, but my mouth wouldn't work. I came to understand how people go mute through trauma.

It was July, just a few months into the Covid-19 lockdown, so added to the grief was that terror we all felt that we might contract the illness, which at the time was killing so many people. Everyone wanted to come see us, but we had to isolate, which only made everything more surreal.

I felt like I had also died. I couldn't eat. I couldn't think. I saw Ben Ben's face in everything everywhere. I couldn't stand up for very long, so I would just lie down most of the time. I felt like I weighed a thousand pounds. A few friends would break Covid protocol and come over and give me baths and shave my legs. All I could manage to do was lie on the floor in the sun.

I was more physically incapacitated than my parents. I had always been the responsible one, in charge and taking control of pretty much everything. But I couldn't this time.

My parents ended up doing all of the arrangements—choosing his coffin, all that. I think they needed to stay busy.

I couldn't even think about it, couldn't hear anything about the arrangements. I remember one day I walked into a room where my mom was smoking a cigarette and looking at different coffins and I turned and walked right back out before she saw me.

I refused to let any of it in.

Ben was such an angel that, to everyone, it felt wrong that he had died. Like a mistake had been made. Even people who spent a short amount of time with him knew he was a force for good. You could sense it emanating off him, like light. It felt like whoever was running this world had just made a colossal error.

There were things about my brother I never knew until he died, which was upsetting to me because we were so close. For one, I'd never heard him sing, but I found a voice note on his phone of him singing and his voice was amazing—rich, gritty, complex, the voice of someone with unseen depths. My mom had a complicated relationship with music and singing, and it wasn't encouraged in our house. I once asked her for singing lessons when I was around eight, and she said, "I think if you can sing, you can sing. I don't think lessons will do anything." Someone had told her that. She didn't want any of her kids to do music to protect us from what she had experienced in her music career.

I didn't know that Ben had ever thought about killing himself. I was gutted that he hadn't shared his pain with me.

My mother and I went through his phone in bed together after he died. We were trying to understand what had happened, to put the pieces together. What time had it happened, who was he talking to? I found an accidental photo he took in the kitchen, presumably while walking back up to his bedroom, just minutes before he died. We found a text sent to my mom a couple of weeks before he died that read, "I think something's wrong with me mentally or something like that. I think I have a mental health issue." It's heartbreaking to me that he only realized he might need help just two weeks before he killed himself. There would have been so much room for him to try to heal his pain. He hadn't even scratched the surface of his struggles. He hadn't tried and failed; he simply hadn't tried yet. He hadn't gone to therapy, not even once. And he certainly hadn't attempted suicide before—no overdose, nothing. No cry for help. The truth is that he hadn't recognized the depth of his depression until it was already too late, and he went straight for a gun. The finality of that was so deeply shattering and confusing.

All we thought about for months after he died were the myriad ways this could have been avoided.

The drinking and drugs had somewhat dulled his imagination, blocked his access to his soul, his light, his connection to creation or God or beauty or hope or whatever the life force is called that adds meaning to our lives. This was something I watched happen over time with my mom, too.

But they hadn't remotely extinguished it. To us, he had felt so alive. He felt joy. He still had his sense of adventure, his humor. Addiction was part of his life, yes, but his desire for joy—his powerful will to live—all that was still there. Visible to everyone around him.

But there was also the effect of my mom's addiction on him.

When Ben died, I thought it would be a matter of hours until my mother relapsed. But she surprised me and remained completely sober to honor him. She really wanted to get her life together and help others somehow. She wanted to be of service.

But she was too broken.

My mom had my brother in the house with us instead

of keeping him at the morgue. They told us that if we could tend to the body, we could have him at home, so she kept him in our house for a while on dry ice. It was really important for my mom to have ample time to say goodbye to him, the same way she'd done with her dad. And I would go and sit in there with him.

My house has a separate casitas bedroom, and I kept Ben Ben in there for two months. There is no law in the state of California that you have to bury someone immediately.

I found a very empathic funeral home owner. I told her that having my dad in the house after he died was incredibly helpful because I could go and spend time with him and talk to him. She said, "We'll bring Ben Ben to you. You can have him there."

"Bring him, then," I said.

We had to keep the room at 55 degrees. I still didn't know where I was going to bury him—Hawaii, Graceland, Hawaii, Graceland—so that was part of why it took so long. But I got so used to him, caring for him and keeping him there.

I think it would scare the living fucking piss out of anybody else to have their son there like that. But not me.

The normal process of death is: The person dies, they have an autopsy, viewing, funeral, buried, boom. It's all over in a four- or five-day period, maybe a week if you're lucky.

But you don't really have a chance to process it. I felt so fortunate that there was a way that I could still parent him, delay it a bit longer so that I could become okay with laying him to rest.

A couple of years before he died, my brother had had the word *Riley* tattooed on his collarbone and *Lisa Marie* tattooed on his hand. After he died, my mom and I had the idea that we should get matching tattoos of his name on the corresponding parts of our bodies. We found a tattoo artist who was able to match Ben's tattoo of my name, and then it came time for him to do my mom's tattoo.

We met with the artist in the little courtyard next to the casitas, and during the meeting my mom became adamant that she wanted her tattoo exactly where my brother had his. The artist said it was possible, but that he'd need to know the font, the positioning.

"Do you happen to have any photos?"

"No," she said, "but I can show you."

I looked at my mom, and with my eyes only, I communicated, *Are you out of your fucking mind? You've never met this guy before. Do not bring him into that room with my dead brother.*

I knew she understood my look, but she plowed ahead.

"He's actually in that room," she said, pointing to the casitas.

Lisa Marie Presley had just asked this poor man to look at the body of her dead son, which happened to be right next to us in the casitas.

I've had an extremely absurd life, but this moment is in the top five.

The tattooist agreed to go in there with us, bless him, and my mom led us into the casitas, opened the casket, and, in the most matter-of-fact way imaginable, proceeded to grab my brother's hand and point out the tattoo, discuss its positioning, show the tattooist where she wanted it on her hand. I stood there aghast, watching him try to engage in the conversation and pretend this was fine. I'm sure he was thinking, *What the fuck is going on?* but he stayed that day and did the tattoo perfectly, right afterward, back in the house.

Soon after that, we all kind of got this vibe from my brother that he didn't want his body in this house anymore. "Guys," he seemed to be saying, "this is getting weird."

Even my mom said that she could feel him talking to her, saying, "This is insane, Mom, what are you doing? What the fuck!"

Ben's funeral was the most brutalizing day of my life.

The service was held in Malibu, overlooking the ocean. I think we broke some Covid rules as over a hundred people came. For the entire car ride there I was shaking so hard I thought I'd shatter or have a heart attack.

We followed the hearse, then watched as his coffin was carried by the pallbearers—all of his closest childhood friends.

The service was as beautiful as it could have been, filled with everything Ben loved. We'd spent half our childhoods in Hawaii, so we had our Hawaiian friend come and play Hawaiian music and bless my brother traditionally. Deepak Chopra led the ceremony. But as beautiful as it all was, I found myself needing to close my eyes simply to be able to bear it. When I'd open them, I could barely see through tears, and what little I did see was a blurry vision of my little sisters in hysterics, gripping on to my mother for dear life. So I'd close them again.

I simply was not there. I had to disassociate, and my spirit left my body again.

I don't remember much other than that I was struggling to stay alive. I was clinging on to all the words Deepak was saying, trying to find some calmness in the moment, but I still felt like I was drowning.

Everyone had written a letter to my brother, and these were attached to biodegradable balloons and sent into the sky as Jeff Buckley's version of Dylan's "I Shall Be Released" played.

It was just punishing.

After that, we sent him to Memphis, to Graceland, to be buried with his grandfather.

And in his casket, I'd quietly placed those yellow Nike sneakers he'd envied when we'd been so happy in Japan.

My family stayed in a house together for six months, in grief together. We'd wake up and all we would talk about, from sunup till sundown, was Ben Ben.

My brother and I were very similar. I always felt like we were twins—our senses of humor, the way we talked, we even sounded like each other. He was just slightly smarter, slightly wittier, and more cerebral. From as early as I can remember we've been able to ask my parents questions like, "What am I doing here, in this world?" and they have always been open to those conversations. So when Ben passed, we had this beautiful grieving experience that I don't think people have very often. We talked about existence and loss and love and their deeper meanings. It was a singular period in which we all felt strongly that we were connecting to something bigger than ourselves. It was my parents, my sisters, my cousins, and my closest friends in a Covid and grief pod. We would take my sisters out into the backyard where we would sing and paint and lie under the stars. It was all Ben-centric, a process led by my mother who said that she wasn't going to let us talk about anything other than her son. I'm really grateful she did that. If I hadn't had her to set that tone, I might have listened to friends urging me to get back to work or move toward a kind of escapism to try to dampen the loss.

My mom simply said, "No, we're experiencing this."

We all agreed that my brother wouldn't have killed himself sober. We all had a sense that the minute he did it, it wasn't truly what he wanted. And knowing that was really hard for us.

I have never been angry with my brother for doing what he did. I feel a tremendous empathy for him, and a profound sadness that he felt, in that moment, that dying was his only solution.

I know in any death there's a feeling of responsibility in the ones left behind, but with suicide, the guilt is deeper. And because he was my little brother, I feel a sense of personal responsibility, like I failed in my role as his big sister. Of course, my parents felt this even more than I did.

I don't fully understand the relationship between free will and destiny, and I accept that. Though I believe my brother didn't truly want to die—and though my parents and I wish we had done things differently to try to avoid this tragedy, and I wish every day to see him again—I have come to believe that everything happens as it's supposed to in that moment. Ben's death somehow solidified that for me. I was in the most pain I've ever been in in my life, but I also had the deeply transformative experience of surrendering to that avalanche of pain and not trying to avoid the grief. This was a huge lesson for me—the only way out is through. You must allow pain in to free yourself from it.

We're told not to cry from the moment we're born. We spend much of our lives trying to disassociate. When we feel something bad we try to make ourselves feel better, because we are afraid of it. Like anyone, I feel uninspired and indifferent about life, and broken at times. Life can be unbearably hard and cruel. But somehow, the loss of my brother reframed all of those moments for me. Ben made me realize that every little thing matters, every little mundane moment, every flash of joy. All the pain.

The loss of my brother made me understand how two things, maybe more than two things, can be true at the same time. This has been one of the most profound experiences I've had. Learning to hold joy and suffering and indifference and hope simultaneously.

Sometimes, even now, I'll be doing something, and grief's volume is turned down so I can (just barely) function, but the rest of the time it's cranked up all the way and I can't hear anything. A childhood friend of mine asked me, "Does it lessen? Does it get any better?" The answer is no. Today I might be able to take a shower and not think about it, tomorrow I could be crying in the shower.

Grief is always there.

Days after he passed, I was sitting with his body in the casitas in hopes that he could somehow help me through the pain I was feeling. That he could give me some guidance through this. And on that day, I swear I could almost hear his voice saying, "There's a point. Keep going."

And that feeling has never left me.

. . .

After Ben Ben died, I knew my mom wouldn't survive it for very long. She did not want to be here.

When he left the casitas, she chose to live the rest of her life in mourning. She wasn't interested in talking about anything other than my brother anymore. She would say that her life was over, that she was only here for her other children, but that she was torn, because she had three children here on earth, but one child somewhere else.

But she really surprised us all. For a start, she didn't relapse. She was more present than she'd been in years, too. She had some incredible moments of living her life in a way that she hadn't in her years of addiction. On our first trip to Hawaii after Ben Ben died, she went snorkeling and swimming in the ocean and hiking and zip-lining. She really tried to hold on to hope, even though it was like sand through her fingers. I could see her trying. She said she was trying. She even tried to reconnect with some of the people she jettisoned when she moved to England. One day she texted me a photo of herself and one of her old friends at lunch—she had called up a few of them and apologized, almost like she was trying to make everything right, to tie up unfinished business here.

And I wish it was all like that, and that I could paint an uplifting, rise-from-the-ashes picture, but the truth is that most days she would sit in her house and smoke a lot of cigarettes and stare out at nothing, at everything.

That's what her grief looked like.

I saw her three times a week and every weekend. If she had it her way, I would have lived with her. And if I missed even an hour on a weekend, she would ask, "What could you possibly be doing?"

She thought about making more music, but she wasn't there yet. More and more she became set on helping people somehow, especially grieving parents. The act of helping was the only way she could feel any relief. She wanted to help others so she could help herself. She would have groups of parents who had also lost children over to her house on Sundays. She would put out little sandwiches, and she and her grief counselor would run grief groups. She wrote an op-ed about grief, the first time she had ever written anything like that. She was planning to do a podcast about grief as a way of finding purpose—she desperately wanted to connect with people who had this shared experience. Nothing else inspired her.

That was what it looked like for my mom to try her hardest to make it for her other kids.

It was beautiful.

My son made me go to Hawaii. I did not want to go. We had a house there, I'd lived there, he loved it there, it was his favorite place. He knew that's where I used to go to heal. Suddenly I found myself planning a trip there, and I said out loud to him, "Okay, this is not me, but I'm going. It's you. I know it's you. I know you know I don't want to go, but I'm going." Then I was there on the actual anniversary of his death. It was not a coincidence, I knew not to invalidate that.

I got some vitamin D. I walked every day for a mile, which was big.

I stopped wanting to die every day.

My daughter, Tupelo, was born in August 2022, and the first week after Tupelo's birth, my mom would come over and do the night shift so Ben and I could sleep, just as I had done for her when she'd had the twins.

My mom instantly became obsessed with Tupelo—she felt she had a special connection with her, so she'd come over to my house in Silver Lake and take her away to be alone with her. I'd watch through the window as they'd go off to sit in the garden—my mom would call it her fairy garden, just as I had called our garden in Hidden Hills a fairy garden for Ben Ben when we were little. My mom bought swing sets and toys that filled her own house so that Tupelo could sleep over.

But despite all this love she still had inside her, and all of her effort to live, we could all see it. We could all feel it coming.

We all knew my mom was going to die of a broken heart.

I'm still only fourteen months out. I'm not crying all day every day, or locking myself in my room all day and not coming out. I've made baby steps. I'm able to have a conversation and not feel like I'm losing my mind. I can think better now. For a long time, I couldn't think at all.

How do I heal? By helping people. One kid wrote to Riley and said, "I didn't kill myself last night because of what you said it would do to my family and those that are left behind. So thank you. I'll find some other way."

That helped me. That brought me up.

You're going to have to find something that's probably nothing that you've done before, and that's going to be your purpose now, like it or not. And you have to follow through. That's what I care about. If I'm honoring my Ben Ben, and if I'm helping other people by sharing the experience I had with him, with addiction or suicide, that feels really authentic to me.

That's where I'm at.

Two years ago, Ben's nanny Uant, who was a grandmother figure to him, emailed all of us and said she was done, that she was going to die. She didn't have anything wrong with her, she was just done. Ben and Riley flew to Florida to have one last visit with her.

But nothing happened. She kept on living. She did that a few times, and Ben and Riley would get all worked up, and then nothing would happen.

About six months ago, I was sitting outside by myself and all of a sudden, I started thinking about Uant. In my head I heard, "I flew all the way to Florida to be with her, go figure. . . ." Memories were coming at me about her, songs she used to sing to Ben Ben when he was little, and I said out loud to Ben, "Okay, sweetheart, I get it. Something with Uant. I get it, I hear you. I got it."

And then I went about my day.

The next morning, Riley came over and said, "Suzanne died last night."

I looked at her.

"Ben Ben told me yesterday," I said. "He was telling me something. I didn't know that's what he was saying. I was talking to him out loud yesterday, saying, 'Okay, something about Uant.' "

I can hear him.

I'm never going to doubt that ever again.

I saw a picture of myself with my parents yesterday. I was five or six. I'm standing between the two of them and they've each got my hand.

I looked at my face as a child and thought, *My God, if only anyone could have told you what you were going to go through in this life, what you were going to be up against.* That cute little blond-haired child in the matching dress with her mommy.

It overwhelmed me.

I'll do that with my own children sometimes. I look at them when they were little, at their faces before they went through the traumas they went through, and I get really sad.

After my father died, people always described me as sad. It was like a permanent imprint on my face after that, in my eyes.

But that sadness was not in this photograph. That forlorn little princess bullshit hadn't reared its ugly head yet.

The sadness started at nine when he passed away, and then it never left. Now it's even worse—my eyes are downcast permanently in this grief. The view is pretty limited.

I always thought, *Why does everybody always say I look sad?*

And now I get it.

I don't think my spark will ever come back, to be perfectly honest. Grief settles. It's not something you overcome. It's something that you live with. You adapt to it. Nothing about you is who you were. Nothing about how or what I used to think is important. The truth is that I don't remember who I was. The other day somebody said, "I know you better than anyone," and I said, "No, you don't. You don't have a fucking clue who I am. Because I don't even know who the fuck I am anymore."

The real me, whoever I had been, detonated completely a year and a half ago.

I have to be okay with it and let it do its thing, let it take me over and consume me, let it ease up on me, let it step on the gas, step on the brake, step on the gas, step on the brake. I'm just driving with it.

If I look back at everything, my whole life, I can just lose it. Try, fail, try, fail, good, bad, fail. I get really overwhelmed and start crying, looking at how fucked up my life has been. Sometimes it feels like there's nothing left, no purpose. Like there's nothing I want to accomplish anymore. No goal, no anything. Zero. I have three remaining children, so I fight it, I fight it, I fight it, I fight it, I fight it. But it's fucking there, alive and well. It's a lion's roar and I have to shut it down, shut it up. I'm surprised I'm still alive. I can't believe I'm still standing. It feels wrong to be alive without Ben.

But then I can look at it another day and think, *Okay, wait, there was that part that wasn't so bad. There was some good over there, and there was some fun over there.* I try to pepper it with, "It's not all just shit. I met this person, that part happened. That was good."

Some of it was good.

Though she was fighting to keep it together for my sisters, my mom's health was deteriorating—she had started to say that her stomach was always bothering her. She would have spells of fevers. She was trying to stay inspired and hold on to hope, but underneath everything, there seemed to be a heartbreak that was only growing. And despite my constant scheduling of appointments, she would never see a doctor.

In 2022 she got an infection and later had to have her uterus removed. It was incredibly hard for her.

"It held all my babies," she said.

One day in October that year, we all went to Disneyland. As we were about to get on a ride she sat down on some stairs and said she didn't feel well, that she was really nauseated. Again, I urged her to go to the doctor, and again, I got no response.

What is the point of an autobiography?

I was thinking my main objective would be to help other people somehow. Or to shed light on something. Make a difference somewhere, somehow. I think people have gone through some of the same things I have, and maybe they'll say, "That really helped me."

That would be fulfilling.

Or maybe people will say, "Holy shit, I can't believe you survived that. I can't believe you're still alive."

When I tell people my stories, they tell me I'm strong. But that makes me crazy because I think, *What's it for, though?* Throw stuff at me and I'll get through it, but for what? What does the strength matter? It doesn't matter to me.

I'm not strong. I am not.

But I am still here. I didn't lose my mind, even though I wanted to. And I could have.

I didn't relapse or die. Or kill myself, which are three things I thought about all day long for the first eight or nine months after Ben Ben died. I've been vacillating between all three.

But I didn't.

I have two little girls that I have to be a mother to. I keep my focus on that. My son was concerned about his sisters. It was his main objective. The few last-moment texts he fired off said to watch and protect his sisters. They don't know this. I won't let them know until they're older.

I know Ben Ben would be infuriated with me if I died and joined him.

He would be mad at me in hell or heaven, wherever we're going.

NINE

MEDITATION GARDEN

The night before my daughter was born, my husband and I and my parents headed out to a Holiday Inn in the Mojave Desert right off the 15 freeway to wait for Tupelo's arrival. Our surrogate was to be induced the following morning. We all had dinner with her—me, my mother and father and husband—then headed back to the hotel.

Next morning, Tupelo was born via C-section. In the rush of it all, I hadn't had time to text or talk to my mom, and I had no idea where she was. But when we were walking the baby to have her Apgar test, we bumped into her. My mom had been looking for us. She wasn't even allowed in the area where we found each other, but in her typical way, she had snuck in and intuitively found her grandchild.

She looked at Tupelo and the first thing she said was, "Ben Ben brought me to you."

When we came home from the hospital, my mom and dad would do the eight P.M. to one A.M. shift together so Ben and I could get some sleep.

They were a few brief months of joy, filled with the new little blessing in our lives. My mom would call Tupelo "our little light," would look in her eyes and say, "Bless her sweet little feisty heart. She's like a fairy-tale creature—a little fawn."

At Thanksgiving, when my sisters, my mom, and I went for a walk outside my mom's house in Calabasas, my mother wouldn't let anyone else hold the baby.

As we walked that day, we discussed our options for Christmas—Tahoe? Utah? Hawaii? To the latter, she said, "Yuck! A hot Christmas is my worst nightmare." Every year she just wanted snow.

At the time I was working in Canada, so I suggested we all head to Whistler in British Columbia. She loved that idea. For the next month I would send her photos of hotels and things to do there. She was really excited about it.

I booked everything for her—flights, hotels, things to do—the bill was astronomical. But she just said, "So what? You never know when it's your last Christmas together."

As the trip approached, all that was left was for her to get her passport renewed.

Then, disaster—despite our best efforts, the passport didn't arrive in time.

As silly as it may seem, not getting to Whistler represented so much to my mother. She was desperate for a magical escape, and Whistler had come to represent an ideal, a dreamland. When it fell through, I swear something changed. She seemed resigned to something, as though she wasn't going to find the joy she once felt here anymore.

On top of her feeling unwell at Disneyland, there was a strange energy at the end of 2022. Unusual things kept happening with her health. She developed an infection and had to go to the hospital in November. There, she was given opioids, which worried me. I didn't want to ask her or police her about it, because I knew this would result in another massive fight. So I trusted that she would take what she needed and not abuse the pills. (After her death, I learned from her toxicology report that she had, in fact, taken a therapeutic amount, and I felt incredibly proud of her.)

Things started cascading. She would constantly complain about her stomach, about feeling nauseated. She would drink lots of Pepto-Bismol, which was always by her bed. I could tell my sisters were worried, too—they'd often ask me, "Is Mama going to be okay?"

I would say yes, but I didn't believe it. I think maybe my sisters knew, too.

After Christmas—a Christmas that did indeed become our last together—we all went to Santa Ynez to ring in 2023. It was no Whistler—it was, in fact, a place we always went for New Year's, so it was more depressing than exciting, but at least we were together. My mom, my sisters, and I took horse rides through the beautiful valley. I watched my mother slowly get into communication with the horse, feel it out, learn its rhythm. She was so in tune with horses—even if the horse was grumpy, she'd find a way to build a relationship with it. It was so moving to watch her intuit a horse's personality.

On New Year's Eve we found ourselves in a honky-tonk bar where a band was doing covers. At one point they did a country version of "Suspicious Minds," and afterward my mom went up to congratulate them. The lead singer was a bit full of himself—he probably liked to look at himself in the backs of spoons—and he barely gave my mom the time of day, which she thought was hilarious.

When she got back to our table she was laughing. "Arrogant son of a bitch," she said.

I said, "I don't think he knew who you were, Mom."

After we finished watching the band, my sisters went to their room, and my mom and I snuck off to a spot next to the nonsmoking hotel restaurant, and giggling like teenagers hiding from their parents, we lit up. I had quit smoking years ago, but I wanted to have this cigarette with my mom. Eventually my dad came around the corner and lit a cigarette, too.

The three of us stood there under the roof, keeping out of the light rain, smoking.

As we smoked, my mother said, "Ugh, that baby—I can't handle her! She fills me up and knocks me dead."

"I know, sweet Sawny," my dad said. (My mom's word "fawn" had become Sawn had become Sawny in our silly shared language.)

There, in that moment, I found myself feeling so grateful that I still had both my parents. I didn't take it for granted.

That was the last time I really hung out with my mom until we had dinner in L.A. together on January 8—coincidentally her father's birthday—just she and I, my husband, and my girlfriends, which was common. She was unusually quiet, withdrawn, in her own world. I kept trying to include her in the conversations, but she looked at me and said, "I'm going to go home."

There was a sadness to her, and the same sense of resignation. I was worried.

My husband and I walked her to her car. She seemed very soft, almost empty, and my mom was not a soft person.

Something had left her.

A couple days later, I went back to Vancouver where I was filming a show. I found myself checking in via text more than usual, but she was less responsive than she normally was. My worry deepened.

On the morning of January 12, my mom texted my dad and said, "Can you please help? My stomach's hurting worse than ever. Can you bring Tums?"

I'd been having a beautiful morning with the baby. I had texted my mom the day before and she hadn't responded, which was really unlike her.

When my dad called, I knew something bad had happened.

"It's your mom," he said, "and it's not looking good."

My heart stopped.

By the time he had gotten to her with the Tums she'd asked for, the housekeeper had found her on the floor.

"They think she's had a heart attack," he said. "She's in an ambulance now. They're trying to resuscitate her."

I went right to the airport and got the first flight I could back to L.A. For the whole car ride, and then while I was in the air, my dad and my husband were texting me.

"They're at the hospital now. . . . She's still alive. . . . They've resuscitated her. . . . She has a pulse now. . . . They're doing a scan to see what happened. . . ."

I had my best friend with me on the plane to help with Tupelo. At some point during the flight, my friend said to me, "People live through heart attacks all the time. . . ."

I looked at her and said, "I don't think she's going to live through it. I don't think she wants to."

We were flying somewhere over Yosemite, and I looked down at the wilderness below covered with snow. Tupelo was screaming and crying by now, and she is not a big crier. Everyone notices that about her, that pretty much all she does is smile. We'll walk through the neighborhood and people will say, "Oh! Look! She's smiling at me!" and I always hold myself back from saying, "It's really nothing personal, she smiles at everyone." But sitting on that crowded plane, I could feel that my baby knew something terrible was happening.

When Tupelo was still in utero, there had been a moment the doctor told us she was underweight. My mom said to me, "Talk to her spirit, tell her to try and gain a little weight. She'll hear you." So I did. I put my hand on my surrogate's belly at lunch one day, and in my mind, I told Tupelo to try and gain a little bit more weight before her birth.

Somehow, she ended up gaining the perfect amount of weight. Maybe it worked.

On the airplane home, I felt like my mother was between two worlds, being resuscitated, falling, resuscitated, falling. I wanted so badly to be there with her—spiritually at least—and tell her that I supported whatever she wanted to do. I closed my eyes and talked to her spirit, just like I had Tupelo's. "If you need to go, go. If you need to stay, stay."

We were somewhere due west of Death Valley when the texts from my dad stopped. I couldn't bear the silence for very long. I texted him, but I already knew.

It was 5:18 P.M. when my father texted, "She's in cardiac arrest again."

Oh God.

At 5:19 he wrote, "Can you call me?"

"No, I'm on the plane," I wrote.

At 5:20 I wrote, "Is she dying?"

My dad didn't respond for four minutes.

I wrote again: "Did she die?"

I waited. Then his reply arrived.

"She passed on a few minutes ago, honey. Didn't want to tell you by text. But I'm worried it's going to hit the papers. I love you so much. I'm really sorry to tell you like this. I don't want you to be blindsided when you get off the plane."

My father was my mom's biggest protector throughout her whole adult life. She had many friends that came and went, but he was there from when she was seventeen until the moment she died. He was the last person with her.

We were still half an hour from L.A. Tupelo had finally calmed enough to sleep a little bit, and I quietly sobbed, trying not to disturb the passengers around me.

The world I'd taken off from in Canada that morning was not the same one I landed in at LAX that night. I didn't recognize this strange new planet. It was already a place that, for two and a half years, had been so painfully empty of my brother, Ben Ben, and now it was empty of my mother, too.

I wondered how many times a heart can break.

As we sped away from the airport, I remember seeing people walking in and out of a brightly lit 7-Eleven. Nothing had changed for them. Of course it had not.

Time did its stretching and contracting thing again. *Here we are again,* I thought. *I know this.*

When my brother died, I was hit with the realization that he was nowhere to be found on Earth. I could travel anywhere and never find him. No matter how far I flew, how far I drove, how far I walked, he was gone. I remember driving through Northern California and passing an immense expanse of empty farmland, and thinking that he wasn't in there, either. He could never be found, no matter how hard I looked.

Now, it was the same feeling with my mother.

She was like a character from the Greek myths—she had human emotions, but she was such a force that sometimes I really thought if she focused hard enough, real thunderbolts would appear. Her power and strength frightened people. She had an uncanny ability to see right into your soul. And she was able to truly, unconditionally love.

She had definitely been reincarnated royal every time. My dad and I would joke that if God had ever asked her to come back *not* as a royal, she would have declined his offer.

My mother was the only person who would say no to God.

. . .

The night before the funeral service, close friends said goodbye to her in the chapel at Graceland.

The next day we held the service at Graceland. All of her friends, everyone who ever loved her, attended, including people she hadn't seen in years, everyone she had jettisoned before she fled to England, just everyone. A choir of her friends sang. What began as an incredibly traumatic and painful morning ended in a celebratory dance party, just like the ones we used to have back in the day—the same people, the same songs.

There was joy.

We all felt she was there.

I couldn't speak, so my husband read my eulogy, "A Letter to My Mama":

> Thank you for being my mother in this life. I am eternally grateful to have spent thirty-three years with you. I am certain I chose the best mother for me in this world, and I knew that as far back as I can remember you. I remember everything. I remember you giving me baths as a baby. I remember you driving me in my car seat, listening to Aretha Franklin. I remember the way you'd cuddle me when I'd come to your bed at night, and the way you smelled.

I remember you taking me for ice cream after school in Florida. I remember you singing me and my brother lullabies at night, and how you'd lay with us until we fell asleep. I remember how, every time you'd leave town, you'd bring me a new tea set from Cracker Barrel.

I remember all the notes you'd leave in my lunch box every day. I remember the feeling I'd get when I'd see you picking me up from school, and the way your hand felt on my forehead. I remember how it felt to be loved by the most loving mother I've ever known. I remember how safe it felt to be in your arms. I remember that feeling as a child and I remember it two weeks ago on your couch.

Thank you for showing me that love is the only thing that matters in this life. I hope I can love my daughter the way you loved me, and the way you loved my brother and my sisters.

Thank you for giving me strength, my heart, my empathy, my courage, my sense of humor, my manners, my temper, my wildness, my tenacity. I am a product of your heart. My sisters are a product of your heart. My brother is a product of your heart. We are you, you are us, my eternal love. I hope you finally know how loved you were here. Thank you for trying so hard for us. If I didn't tell you every day, thank you.

The service ended and night fell. My mom's casket was laid across a golf cart, just like the one her father had given her decades ago, the one that had given her her first taste of freedom. All of her closest friends and loved ones followed the golf cart and walked my mother from the chapel to the Meditation Garden in the backyard of Graceland.

We laid her to rest next to my brother, across from her father.

AFTERWORD

About a week before this book was first published, I was at home with my husband and daughter, eating dinner and then sitting on the couch. It was a warm night. We got Tupelo to bed, Ben went off to do some things around the house, and I felt compelled to go to my bedroom, though I wasn't tired. I put my phone away and lay on top of the bed for a few minutes before realizing that I had come here to listen for something, to look for anything, a sign of my mother. Something you're always afraid to look for in the event that it's not there. I closed my eyes and tried to find her, thinking back to when I had lain right here listening to her tapes for the first time, but saw nothing, heard nothing.

The room was empty. I was here, alone.

"I hope this is how you wanted this all to happen," I said to her, to nobody.

Only a deep silence.

. . .

And then, suddenly, she was everywhere.

She was on magazine covers and TV shows. She was all over social media. Clips of my mother's disembodied voice were playing as podcast teasers. I took Oprah around Graceland and showed her my mother's favorite places to get in trouble.

I went around the country talking about her endlessly. I was at Graceland talking about her onstage with my grandmother. I was in New York, Los Angeles, Nashville, St. Louis, talking about the contours of her life, about how painful the writing process had been for her while she was alive and then how painful the writing process had been for me in finishing it. The whole time, all I could think about was what she would have wanted. I knew, above all else, that she would have wanted the book to be authentic. After that, she would have wanted to feel like people really knew her, to finally be in control of her story. She would have wanted people to understand her grief, pain, joy, everything.

Everywhere I went, I looked for a sign of her telling me that she was happy with my choice to complete the book. Or that she was around at all. One interviewer asked me what my mother's favorite books were, and

I immediately thought of the well-read, dog-eared copy of Laura Lynne Jackson's *Signs* that sat on her kitchen table. "It shouldn't be that surprising that this book about communicating with loved ones who have passed away was one of my mom's favorites. It was a staple in her house," I said. I think I'm always open to something magical happening. I value magical thinking. I think it's important to keep a hold of childlike wonder. But in this moment, I had to come to the stark realization that she had truly missed it all.

After I had finished the book tour and all the media surrounding the book, after I'd talked about my mother and our family publicly more in a month than I had cumulatively in my entire life, I went back home and tried to process what had just happened. I talked to my father about how he felt about the book, its publication. We agreed that even though she hadn't been able to finish the book, she still felt like a far more complete picture than she had before.

I heard from people who had read the book and felt compelled to write and tell me how they felt. Many of the letters and responses brought me to tears because they were so touching, but also because they were exactly the reaction that I know my mother had wanted to elicit. If she could make just one person feel less alone, less imprisoned in grief or depression, that would have been enough for her. She told me that. As I read through the reactions, I tried to imagine her reading them over my shoulder, as the world for once embraced her lovingly, in all of her glory and pain and defects and triumphs.

Life started to get back to normal. The whole experience started to feel like it had been some kind of fever dream, like I had been walking through preordained steps that had been set up by someone else, to be walked by yet another.

That concept started to hit me so deeply that it caused me to look back on my life and wonder if it was all predetermined. I had always been a writer and one of my roles in our family had been documentarian. When I was younger, my mom would always tell me I'm going to make a documentary about her one day. Was the book always meant to go this way? Was everything? Had I entered this life to document hers? Without any word from her, I felt like I was starting to spin out.

I like to imagine that people who have passed away still get the opportunity to watch their loved one's lives unfold. Not because I've seen any proof of it, just because I like the idea. But what if she doesn't see anything. What if when people die, they're just gone?

What if a sign from her never came?

These were the ever-loudening thoughts swirling in my head when our second child was born two weeks early, on February 1.

My mother's birthday.

—Riley Keough

ACKNOWLEDGMENTS

Thank you to Cait Hoyt, Ben Greenberg, Luke Dempsey, David Kuhn, Neil Strauss, Alexandra Trustman, Maha Dakhil, Steve Warren, Jennifer Gray, Hilary McClellen, Angie Marchese, Roger Widynowski, and Danny Keough.

IMAGE CREDITS

ABOUT THE AUTHORS

LISA MARIE PRESLEY was a singer and songwriter who was born in Memphis and raised at Graceland as the only child of Elvis and Priscilla Presley. She released three studio albums throughout her music career—*To Whom It May Concern, Now What,* and *Storm & Grace,* the first of which was certified gold. Lisa Marie passed away in January 2023.

RILEY KEOUGH is an Emmy, Golden Globe, and Independent Spirit Award–nominated actress. She is known for her work in *Daisy Jones & the Six, Zola,* and more. She also co-directed *War Pony* (2022), which won the Caméra d'Or for best first feature film at Cannes, and cofounded the production company Felix Culpa with Gina Gammell. She is the eldest daughter of Lisa Marie Presley and sole trustee of Graceland.

ABOUT THE TYPE

This book was set in Minion, a 1990 Adobe Originals typeface by Robert Slimbach. Minion is inspired by classical, old-style typefaces of the late Renaissance, a period of elegant and beautiful type designs. Created primarily for text setting, Minion combines the aesthetic and functional qualities that make text type highly readable with the versatility of digital technology.